KINDERGARTEN
K
AGES 5-6

Kindergarten
Big Fun Workbook

For information about permission to reproduce selections from this book for
an entire school or school district, please contact permissions@highlights.com.

Published by Highlights Press • 815 Church Street • Honesdale, Pennsylvania 18431
ISBN: 978-1-62979-763-2
Mfg. 04/2020
Printed in Mattoon, IL, USA
First edition
10 9 8 7 6

For assistance in the preparation of this book, the editors would like to thank:
Vanessa Maldonado, MSEd; MS Literacy Ed. K–12; Reading/LA Consultant Cert.; K–5 Literacy Instructional Coach
Kristin Ward, MS Curriculum, Instruction, and Assessment; K–5 Mathematics Instructional Coach
Jump Start Press, Inc.

It's Time for Big Fun!

The pages of this book are filled with hundreds of curriculum-based puzzles and activities to help your child succeed in kindergarten—in areas such as the alphabet, sight words, rhyming, opposites, counting, addition, subtraction, colors, shapes, grouping and sorting, and patterns.

How to use this book:

1 **Find the right time.**
Your kindergartener may be tired and hungry after school, so you may want to wait to introduce a new activity when she is well fed and rested.

2 Let your child take the lead.
There is no one "right way" to do this book. Let your child select the activities that interest him most and do them at a pace that works for him.

3 Set a good example.
Try sitting down with your child to do some of your own "work" while your child does her activities. This way, you'll be right there to guide her if she needs it.

4 Pour on the praise.
When your child works hard to complete a page, acknowledge his efforts enthusiastically.

5 Encourage cooperation and teamwork.
If you see your child struggling with a concept, offer to work together as a team. Give her clues if you like, but don't provide answers for her.

Contents

Home, Sweet Home

Trace the path to help the bee get to its hive.

Trace the path to help the beaver get to its lodge.

Emergent Writing: Fine Motor Skills

Yum!

Trace each straw to help these kids drink their ice-cream sodas.

Play Ball!

Trace each line to show the way the ball moves.

Draw your own line here.

Flower Fun

Trace the lines from the flowers to the ground.
Which flower is yellow?

Write Your Name

What's your name? Practice writing it.

This backpack belongs to:

(write your name)

Draw a design on this backpack!

Self-Portrait

Draw a picture of yourself.

Say 3 things you like about yourself.

This is a picture of _____

(write your name)

Aa

This is an uppercase A.

This is a lowercase a.

Trace the uppercase **A**. Then write your own.

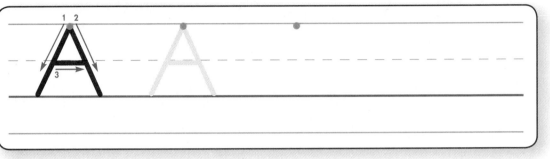

Trace the lowercase **a**. Then write your own.

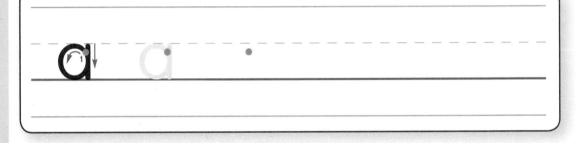

Now trace **A** and **a** to finish the sentence.

Alice picks

apples.

Say the name of this picture.

The word **apple** begins with the short **a** sound.

Circle the pictures that start with the same sound.

Say the name of this picture.

The word **ape** begins with the long **a** sound.

Circle the pictures that start with the same sound.

Awesome Acrobats

Phonics: Short a and Long a

Find and circle **8** objects that begin with the letter **a** in this Hidden Pictures® puzzle.

arrow

ax

acorn

alligator

ant

apple

artist's brush

airplane

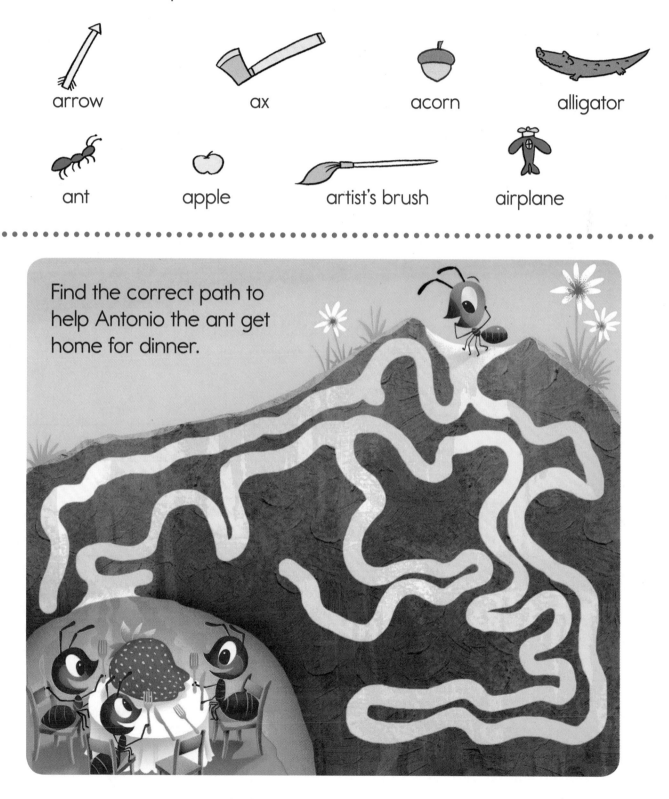

Find the correct path to help Antonio the ant get home for dinner.

Bb

This is an uppercase B.

This is a lowercase b.

Trace the uppercase **B**. Then write your own.

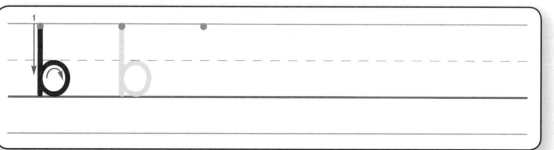

Trace the lowercase **b**. Then write your own.

Now trace **B** and **b** to finish the sentence.

Ben

has a

balloon.

Say the name of this picture.

The word **balloon** begins with the **b** sound.

Circle the pictures that start with the same sound.

Find the 2 birds that look the same.

Bears Everywhere!

Giant bears, tiny bears
Bears in every size
Scruffy bears
Fluffy bears
Bears with button eyes
Bears in boots and
    bathing suits
But just one bear is right—
A bear to hug,
    a bear to love
My bear to kiss good night.

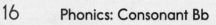

How many **B**'s can you find in this picture? How many bears can you find? Look for things that start with the **B** sound.

Cc

This is an uppercase C.

This is a lowercase c.

Trace the uppercase **C**. Then write your own.

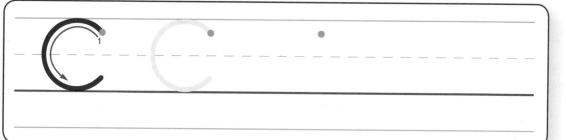

Trace the lowercase **c**. Then write your own.

Now trace **C** and **c** to finish the sentence.

Cara

makes

cupcakes.

Say the name of this picture.

The word **candle** begins with the hard **c** sound.

Circle the pictures that start with the same sound.

Draw more cars on this road.

C Is For?

Phonics: Consonant Cc

Can you find a cat, a cow, and a castle?
What other things can you find that begin with the letter **c**?

Dd

This is an uppercase D.

This is a lowercase d.

Trace the uppercase **D**. Then write your own.

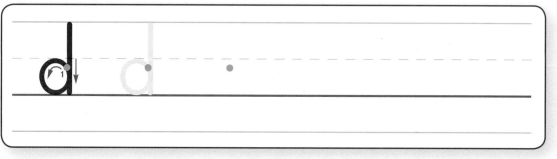

Trace the lowercase **d**. Then write your own.

Now trace **D** and **d** to finish the sentence.

Dan walks

his dog.

Say the name of this picture.

The word **dog** begins with the **d** sound.

Circle the pictures that start with the same sound.

Color the dolphins.

A Day at the Dog Park

Dogs in the dog park
Love to run.
Big ones, small ones
Join the fun.

Round and round
And up and over—
There goes Rusty,
There goes Rover.

Anytime, any day,
Dogs in the dog park
Love to play!

How many
D's can you find?

How many big dogs
do you see?

How many small dogs
do you see?

What else do
you see?

Ee

This is an uppercase E.

This is a lowercase e.

Trace the uppercase **E**. Then write your own.

Trace the lowercase **e**. Then write your own.

Now trace **E** and **e** to finish the sentence.

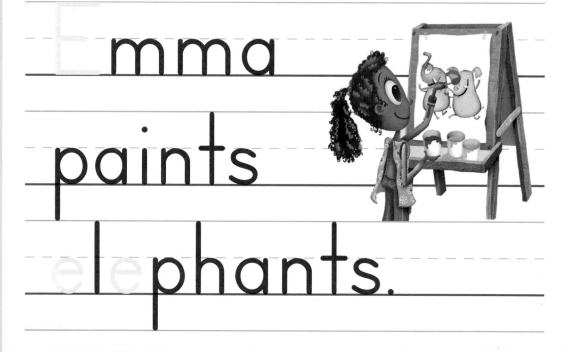

Emma paints elephants.

Say the name of this picture.

The word **egg** begins with the short **e** sound.

Circle the pictures that start with the same sound.

• •

Say the name of this picture.

The word **eagle** begins with the long **e** sound.

Circle the pictures that start with the same sound.

Eggs for Everyone

Find and circle **8** objects that begin with the letter **e** in this Hidden Pictures® puzzle.

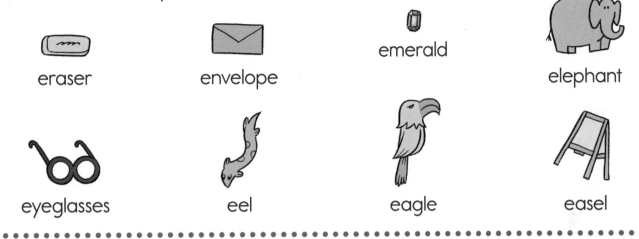

eraser

envelope

emerald

elephant

eyeglasses

eel

eagle

easel

Follow the steps to draw an elephant, or draw one from your imagination.

1

2

3

Ff

This is an uppercase F.

This is a lowercase f.

Trace the uppercase **F**. Then write your own.

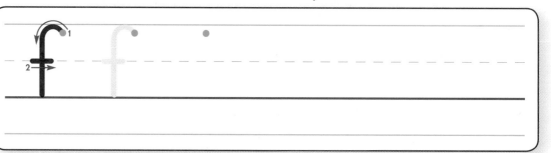

Trace the lowercase **f**. Then write your own.

Now trace **F** and **f** to finish the sentence.

Finn catches a fish.

Say the name of this picture.

The word **fork** begins with the **f** sound.

Circle the pictures that start with the same sound.

Draw a picture of an animal who lives on this farm.

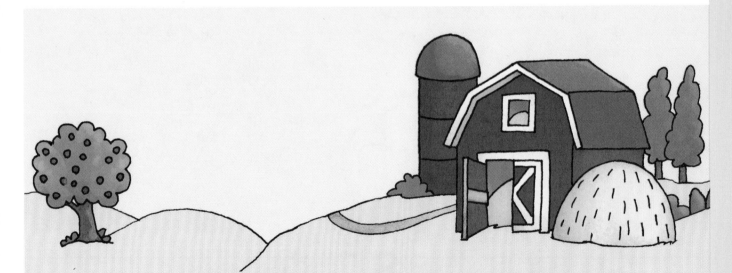

The Fly and the Frog

Felix the fly flew
right past her,
But Felicity's tongue
was much faster.
Fortunately for Felicity,
Felix wasn't a bee.
A stung tongue would
have been
a disaster.

Phonics: Consonant Ff

Gg

This is an uppercase G.

This is a lowercase g.

Trace the uppercase **G**. Then write your own.

Trace the lowercase **g**. Then write your own.

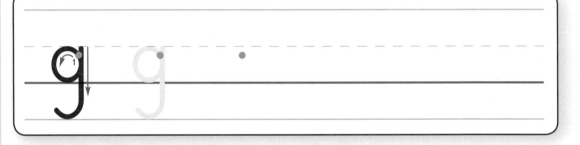

Now trace **G** and **g** to finish the sentence.

Gabi
likes
grapes.

Say the name of this picture.

The word **goat** begins with the hard **g** sound.

Circle the pictures that start with the same sound.

Draw a line from each giraffe to its match.

G Is For?

Phonics: Consonant Gg

Can you find a goose, a gorilla, and a gate?
What other things can you find that begin with the letter g?

Knock, knock.
Who's there?
Goat.
Goat who?
Goat to the door
and find
out!

Hh

This is an uppercase **H**.

This is a lowercase **h**.

Trace the uppercase **H**. Then write your own.

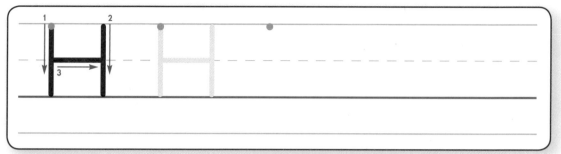

Trace the lowercase **h**. Then write your own.

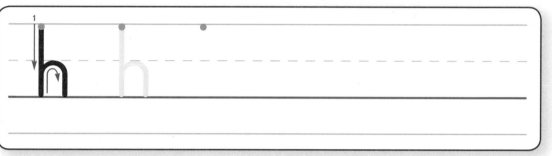

Now trace **H** and **h** to finish the sentence.

Hugo

rides a

horse.

Say the name of this picture.

The word **house** begins with the **h** sound.

Circle the pictures that start with the same sound.

Color these hats. Which one would you like to wear?

Hannah's Hairbrush

Phonics: Consonant Hh

Find and circle **8** objects that begin with the letter **h** in this Hidden Pictures® puzzle.

heart   hamburger   hockey stick   horn

hot dog   handbag   hammer   horseshoe

Find and circle the thing that is different on each hippo.

Ii

This is an uppercase I.

This is a lowercase i.

Trace the uppercase **I**. Then write your own.

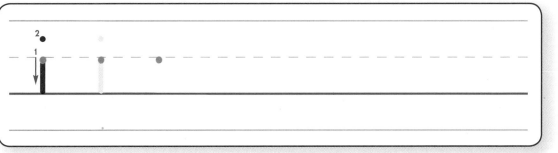

Trace the lowercase **i**. Then write your own.

Now trace **I** and **i** to finish the sentence.

Issac

likes

ice cream.

Say the name of this picture.

The word **igloo** begins with the short **i** sound.

Circle the picture that starts with the same sound.

· ·

Say the name of this picture.

The word **ice** begins with the long **i** sound.

Circle the pictures that start with the same sound.

I Scream "Ice Cream!"

Phonics: Short i and Long i

How are these pictures the same? How are they different?
How many I's can you find in this picture?

Jj

This is an uppercase J.

This is a lowercase j.

Trace the uppercase **J**. Then write your own.

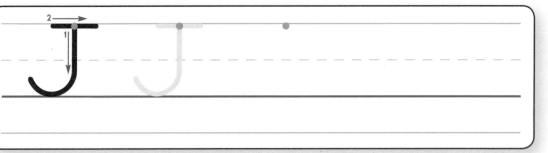

Trace the lowercase **j**. Then write your own.

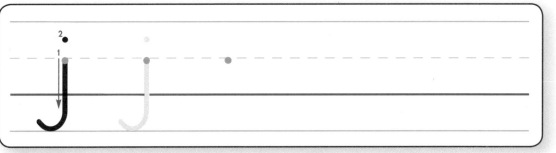

Now trace **J** and **j** to finish the sentence.

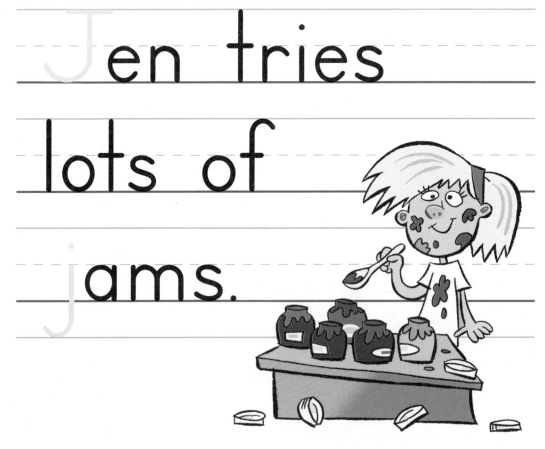

Jen tries lots of jams.

Say the name of this picture.

The word **jam** begins with the **j** sound.

Circle the pictures that start with the same sound.

Color these jackets. What color is your jacket?

Juggling Jesters

Phonics: Consonant Jj

Find and circle **8** objects that begin with the letter **j** in this Hidden Pictures® puzzle.

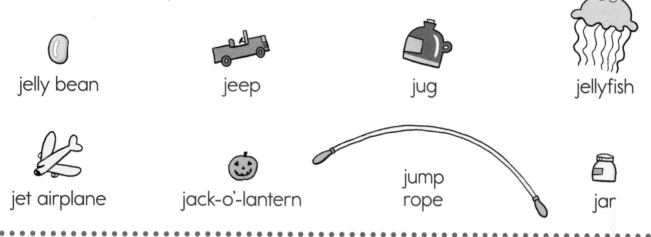

jelly bean

jeep

jug

jellyfish

jet airplane

jack-o'-lantern

jump
rope

jar

Find the 2 juice boxes that look the same.

Kk

This is an uppercase K.

This is a lowercase k.

Trace the uppercase **K**. Then write your own.

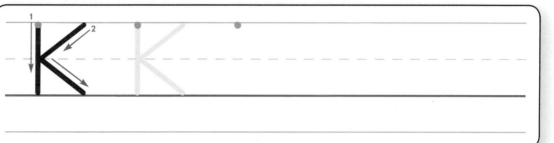

Trace the lowercase **k**. Then write your own.

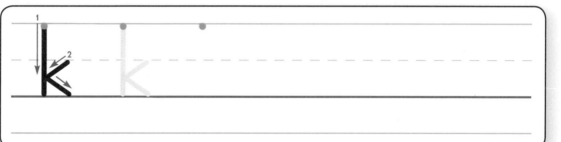

Now trace **K** and **k** to finish the sentence.

Kevin

flies a

kite.

Say the name of this picture.

The word **koala** begins with the **k** sound.

Circle the pictures that start with the same sound.

· ·

Draw a line from each kangaroo to its match.

Kooky K's

A kitten in a kayak flying a kite.
A kid wearing khakis riding a bike.
A kiwi in a kilt playing a kazoo.
Can any of these kooky things possibly be true?

Phonics: Consonant Kk

How many **K**'s can you find in this picture? Can you find each thing in the poem? Look for other things that start with the **K** sound.

Knock, knock.
Who's there?
Kanga.
Kanga who?
Kangaroo,
silly!

Ll

This is an uppercase L.

This is a lowercase l.

Trace the uppercase **L**. Then write your own.

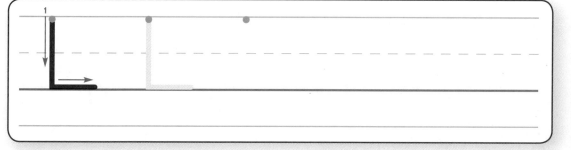

Trace the lowercase **l**. Then write your own.

Now trace **L** and **l** to finish the sentence.

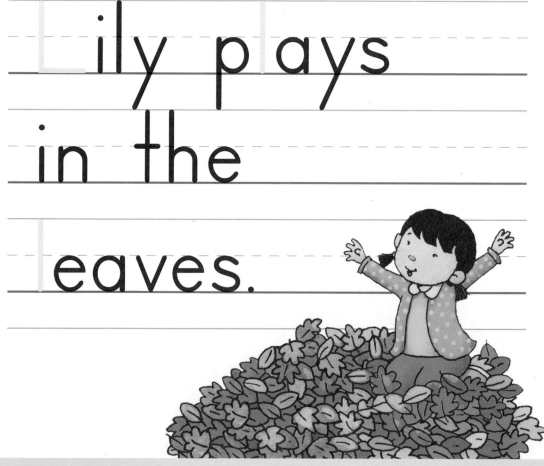

Lily pays in the leaves.

Say the name of this picture.

The word **leaf** begins with the **l** sound.

Circle the pictures that start with the same sound.

Draw a picture of what this lion is roaring at.

L Is For?

Phonics: Consonant Ll

Can you find a lock, a lamp, and a lion?
What other things can you find that begin with the letter l?

Mm

This is an uppercase M.

This is a lowercase m.

Trace the uppercase **M**. Then write your own.

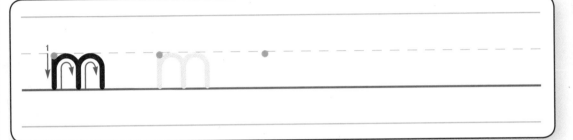

Trace the lowercase **m**. Then write your own.

Now trace **M** and **m** to finish the sentence.

Max

checks the

mailbox.

Say the name of this picture.

The word **mushroom** begins with the **m** sound.

Circle the pictures that start with the same sound.

Draw a line from each monster to its match.

Moose Munch

When moose go meandering in the
marshy muck,
I wonder if their feet ever get stuck.
Do moose mind getting muddy
as they munch on tender shoots?
I may be mistaken, but I think
they might need boots!

How many M's can you find in this picture?

Nn

This is an uppercase N.

This is a lowercase n.

Trace the uppercase **N**. Then write your own.

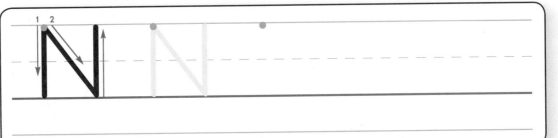

Trace the lowercase **n**. Then write your own.

Now trace **N** and **n** to finish the sentence.

Nate eats

noodles.

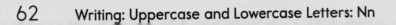

Say the name of this picture.

The word **newspaper** begins with the **n** sound.

Circle the pictures that start with the same sound.

Draw a picture of what's in this nest.

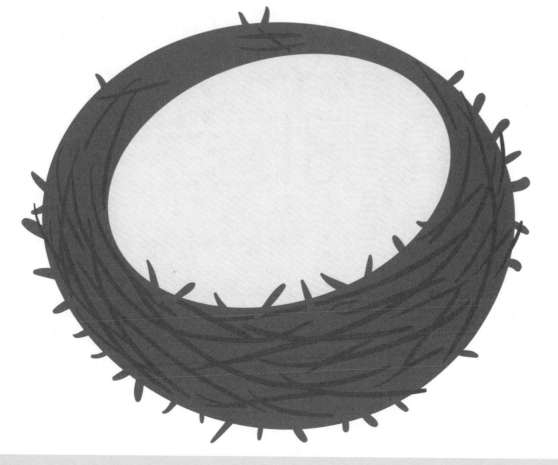

Neat Newts

Phonics: Consonant Nn

Find and circle **8** objects that begin with the letter **n** in this Hidden Pictures® puzzle.

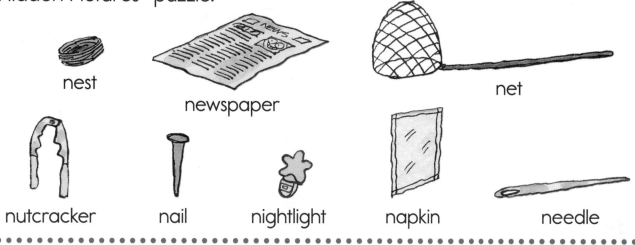

nest

newspaper

net

nutcracker

nail

nightlight

napkin

needle

Trace each path to see which squirrel gets which nut.

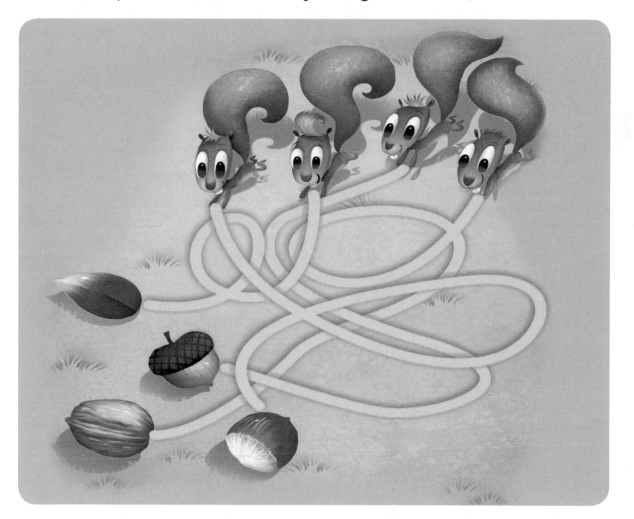

 Oo

This is an uppercase O.

This is a lowercase o.

Trace the uppercase O. Then write your own.

Trace the lowercase o. Then write your own.

Now trace O and o to finish the sentence.

Olivia likes

oranges.

Say the name of this picture.

The word olive begins with the short o sound.

Circle the pictures that start with the same sound.

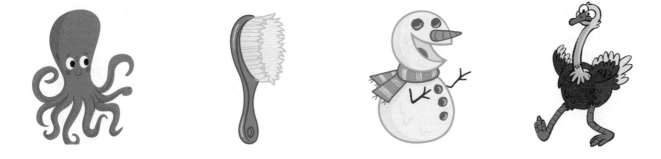

Say the name of this picture.

The word ocean begins with the long o sound.

Circle the picture that starts with the same sound.

Otto's Garage

How many O's can you find in this picture?

Phonics: Short o and Long o

Owl Match

Draw a line from each owl to its match.

Pp

This is an uppercase P.

This is a lowercase p.

Trace the uppercase **P**. Then write your own.

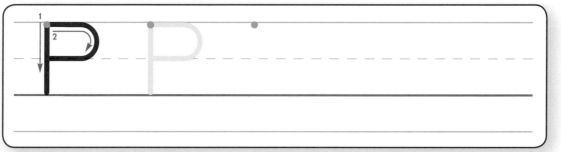

Trace the lowercase **p**. Then write your own.

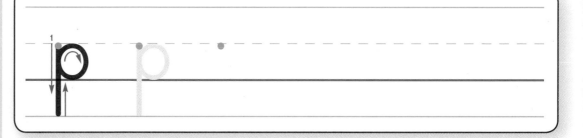

Now trace **P** and **p** to finish the sentence.

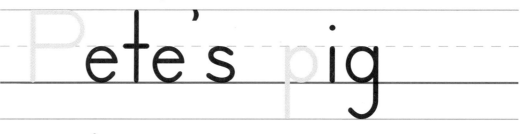

Pete's pig wins.

Say the name of this picture.

The word **pencil** begins with the **p** sound.

Circle the pictures that start with the same sound.

Draw a line between the 2 pianos that look the same.

P Is For?

Phonics: Consonant Pp

Can you find a pig, a pizza, and a puppy?
What other things can you find that begin with the letter **p**?

Knock, knock.
Who's there?
Peas.
Peas who?
Peas open
the door!

Qq

This is an uppercase Q.

This is a lowercase q.

Trace the uppercase **Q**. Then write your own.

Trace the lowercase **q**. Then write your own.

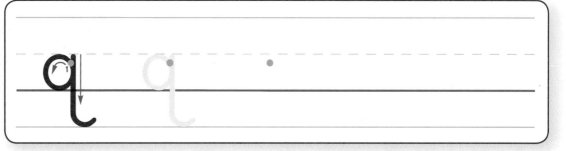

Now trace **Q** and **q** to finish the sentence.

Quinn's quilt is soft.

Say the name of this picture.

The word **queen** begins with the **q** sound.

Circle the pictures that start with the same sound.

Draw a design on this quilt.

Quincy's Quilt

Quincy is making a quilt. Look at the pattern of squares in each row across. Draw a line from each square in Quincy's hands to the place it should go on the quilt.

The Queen's Throne

Follow the **Q**'s to help the queen get back to her throne.

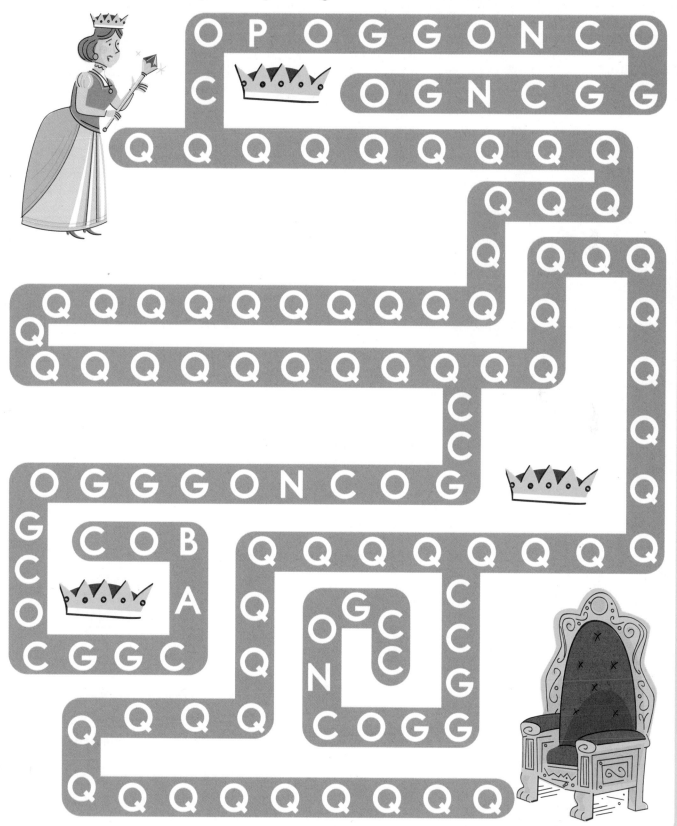

Rr

This is an uppercase R.

This is a lowercase r.

Trace the uppercase **R**. Then write your own.

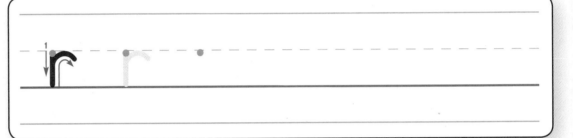

Trace the lowercase **r**. Then write your own.

Now trace **R** and **r** to finish the sentence.

Russ loves to read.

Say the name of this picture.

The word **raccoon** begins with the **r** sound.

Circle the pictures that start with the same sound.

.....

Draw the missing parts of these robots.

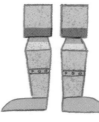

Recess Riddles

Climb the steps up to the sky.
Down, down, down. How fast you'll fly!
What am I?

I can spin fast or sometimes slow.
Hop up. Hold on. Now here we go!
What am I?

I can fly high.
Up, up I swoop.
I whirl, I twirl,
I loop-the-loop!
What am I?

PARK

The picture can help you solve the riddles. How many **R**'s can you find in this picture?

Ss

This is an uppercase S.

This is a lowercase s.

Trace the uppercase **S**. Then write your own.

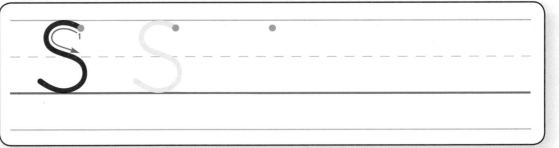

Trace the lowercase **s**. Then write your own.

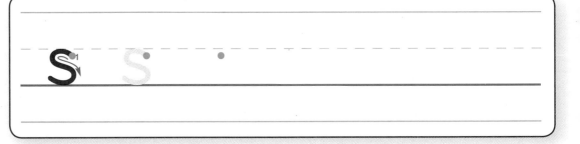

Now trace **S** and **s** to finish the sentence.

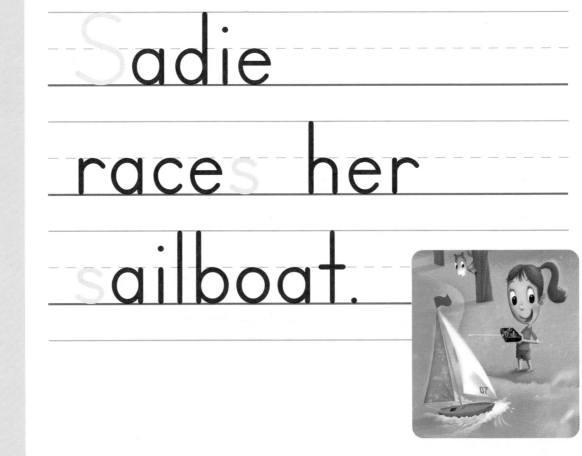

Sadie races her sailboat.

Say the name of this picture.

The word **sock** begins with the **s** sound.

Circle the pictures that start with the same sound.

Draw a line from each sandwich to its match.

School Surprise

Phonics: Consonant Ss

Find and circle **8** objects that begin with the letter **s** in this Hidden Pictures® puzzle.

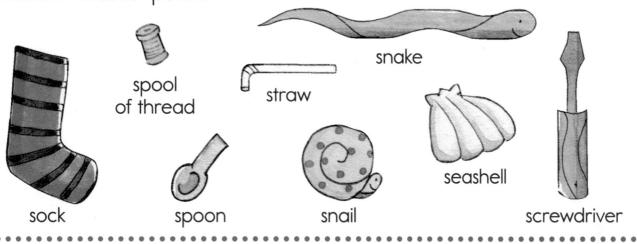

spool
of thread

snake

straw

seashell

sock

spoon

snail

screwdriver

Draw a smile on this silly snowman. What things do you see that start with the letter **s**?

Tt

This is an uppercase T.

This is a lowercase t.

Trace the uppercase **T**. Then write your own.

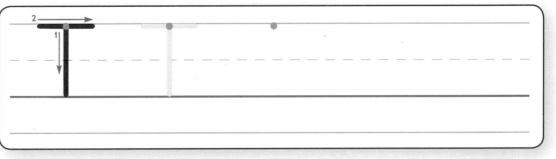

Trace the lowercase **t**. Then write your own.

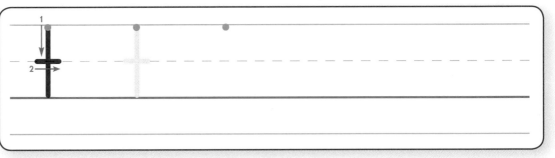

Now trace **T** and **t** to finish the sentence.

Tamika

has

tools.

Say the name of this picture.

The word **table** begins with the **t** sound.

Circle the pictures that start with the same sound.

Draw some stripes on this tiger.

T Is For?

Phonics: Consonant Tt

Can you find a toothbrush, a tiger, and a tree?
What other things can you find that begin with the letter t?

Knock, knock.
Who's there?
Tree.
Tree who?
Tree more days
'til vacation!

U u

This is an uppercase U.

This is a lowercase u.

Trace the uppercase **U**. Then write your own.

Trace the lowercase **u**. Then write your own.

Now trace **U** and **u** to finish the sentence.

Una's

umbrella

is open.

Say the name of this picture.

The word **uncle** begins with the short **u** sound.

Circle the picture that starts with the same sound.

Say the name of this picture.

The word **unicorn** begins with the long **u** sound.

Circle the pictures that start with the same sound.

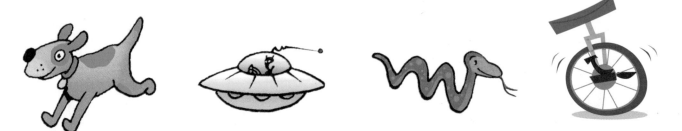

Umbrella Search

Can you find 10 umbrellas in this scene?

Phonics: Short u and Long u

Unique Unicycles

How are these unicyclists the same? How are they different?

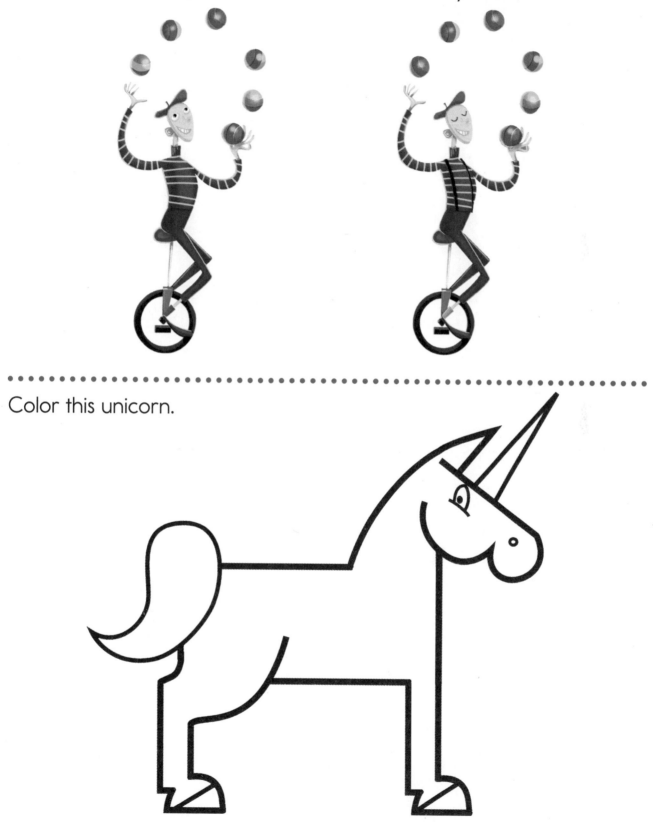

Color this unicorn.

Vv

This is an uppercase V.

This is a lowercase v.

Trace the uppercase V. Then write your own.

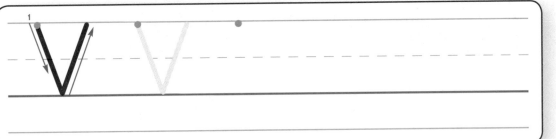

Trace the lowercase v. Then write your own.

Now trace V and v to finish the sentence.

Vinnie plays the violin.

Say the name of this picture.

The word **vest** begins with the **v** sound.

Circle the pictures that start with the same sound.

Trace the paths to see which vacuum cleaner is plugged into which outlet.

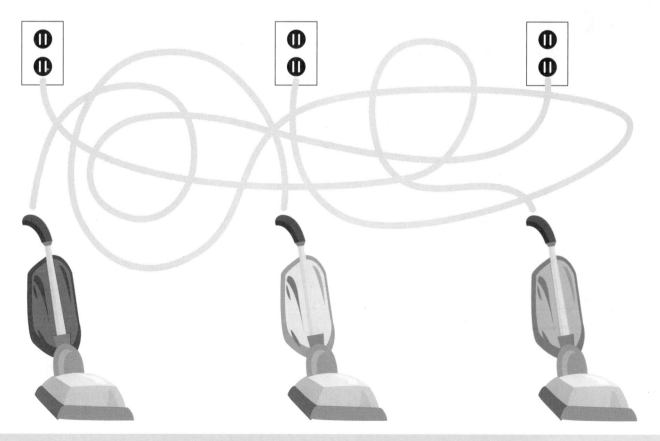

Victor Vole's Magic

Victor Vole, in velvet vest, Does magic tricks in Spanish. His very best trick comes at lunch. He makes his veggies vanish!

How many V's can you find in this picture?

My Very Own Vase

Draw a design on this vase.

Ww

This is an uppercase W.

This is a lowercase w.

Trace the uppercase **W**. Then write your own.

W W W

Trace the lowercase **w**. Then write your own.

w w w

Now trace **W** and **w** to finish the sentence.

Wendy

pulls

a wagon.

Say the name of this picture.

The word **whale** begins with the **w** sound.

Circle the pictures that start with the same sound.

Draw a picture of what you see outside the window.

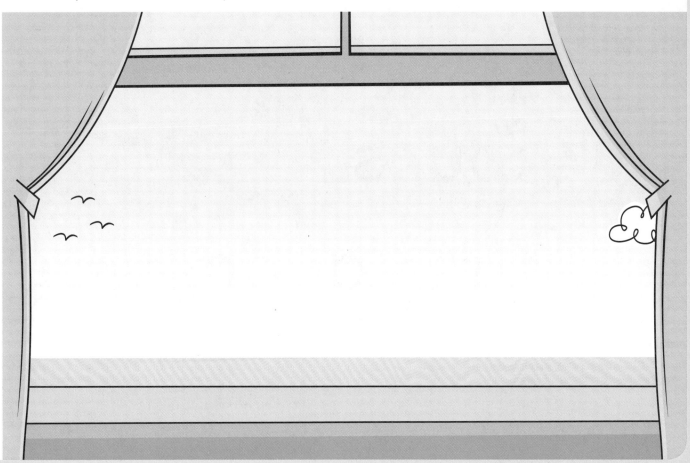

Worm School

Wandering worms will
sometimes wiggle
into a wacky curlicue.
But when those same worms
go to school, they learn
to form a **W**.

Phonics: Consonant Ww

How many **W**'s can you find in this picture?

Trace the worms with your finger. What other letters do you think these worms could make?

Xx

This is an uppercase X.

This is a lowercase x.

Trace the uppercase **X**. Then write your own.

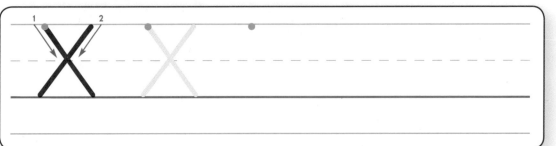

Trace the lowercase **x**. Then write your own.

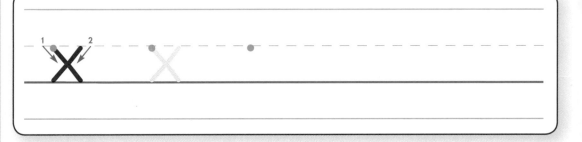

Now trace **X** and **x** to finish the sentence.

Xavier plays the saxophone.

Say the name of this picture.

The word **box** ends with the **x** sound.

Circle the picture that ends with the same sound.

Follow the **X**'s to help the fox get to his mama.

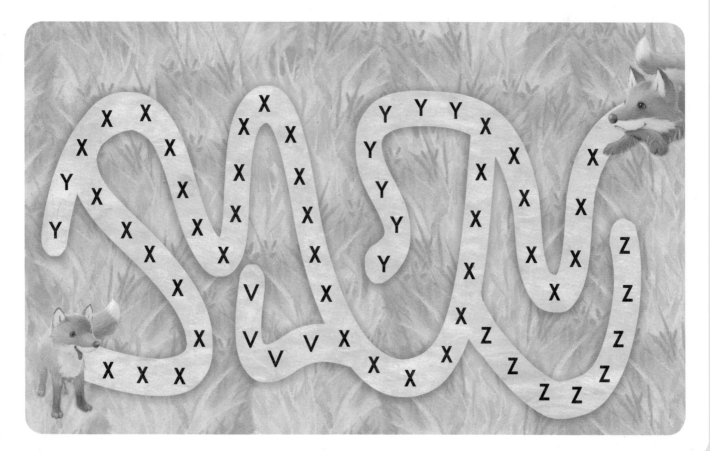

Double X-Rays

Find and circle **6** differences between these 2 X-rays.

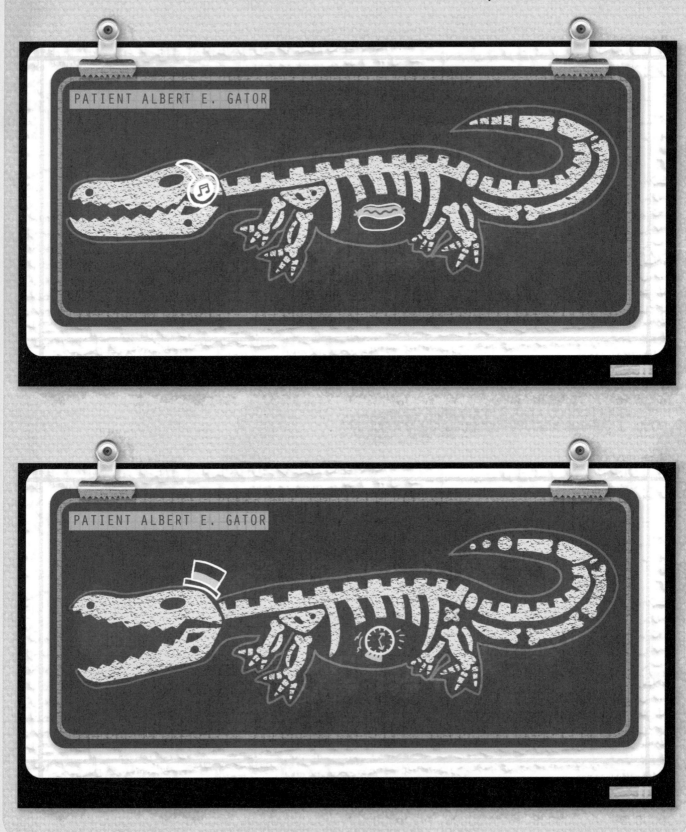

Phonics: Consonant Xx

Fox's Box

Draw a picture of what's in Fox's box.

Yy

This is an uppercase Y.

This is a lowercase y.

Trace the uppercase **Y**. Then write your own.

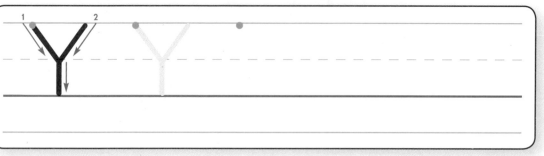

Trace the lowercase **y**. Then write your own.

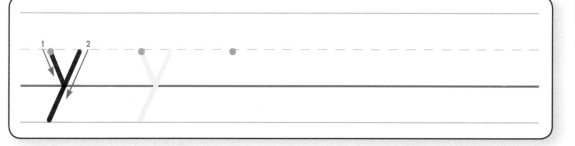

Now trace **Y** and **y** to finish the sentence.

Yolanda knits with yarn.

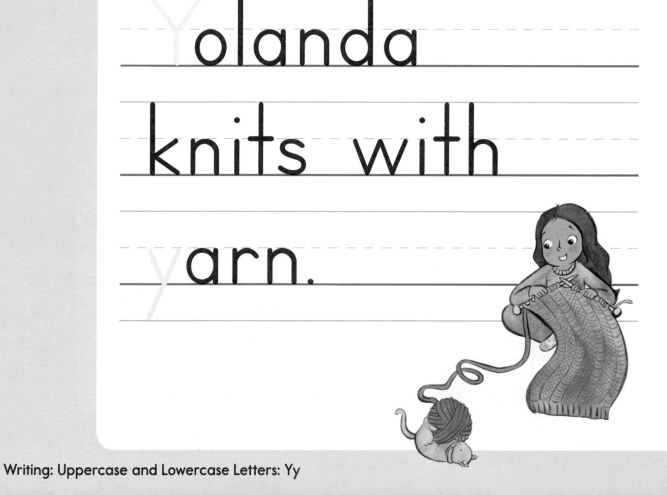

Say the name of this picture.

The word **yak** begins with the **y** sound.

Circle the pictures that start with the same sound.

Draw a line from each yogurt cup to its match.

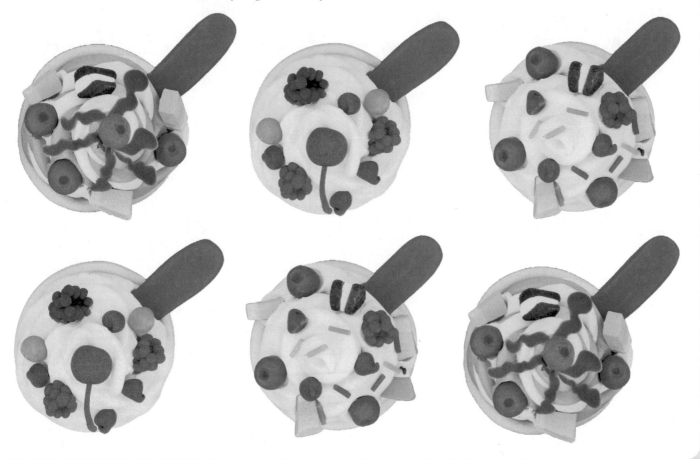

Yo-Yo Search

Find and circle 5 hidden yo-yos in this picture.

Phonics: Consonant Yy

Wacky Yaks

These yaks mixed up their shoes. Match each yak with the right pair of shoes.

Zz

This is an uppercase Z.

This is a lowercase z.

Trace the uppercase Z. Then write your own.

Trace the lowercase z. Then write your own.

Now trace Z and z to finish the sentence.

Zoe's vest
has 5
zippers.

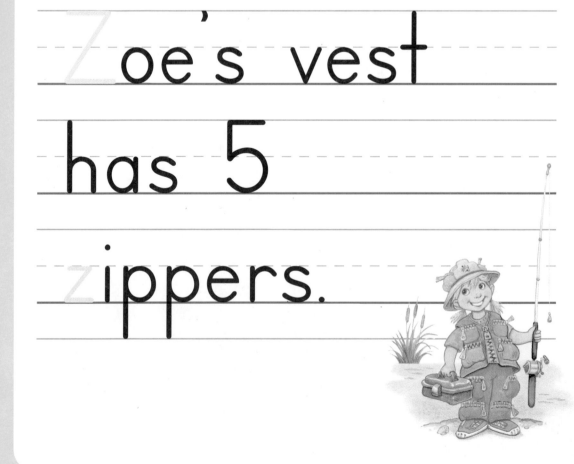

Say the name of this picture.

The word **zebra** begins with the **z** sound.

Circle the pictures that start with the same sound.

Draw some stripes on this zebra.

Zebra Maze

Follow the Z's to help the baby zebra get to its mom.

Z   Z   Z   Z   F   F
                    F   F
                Z
            X   X   X   F
                             F
Z   Z   Z   Z   Z   F

Z
                S
Z
                S

Z   Z   Z   Z   Z   Z

Phonics: Consonant Zz

Zipper Search

Can you find **10** zippers in this scene?

Letter Match-Up

Match the uppercase letter to the lowercase letter.

A   ○   ○ c

M   ○   ○ q

J   ○   ○ f

F   ○   ○ j

Q   ○   ○ m

Y   ○   ○ y

C   ○   ○ a

Print Concepts: Recognize Uppercase and Lowercase Letters

Match the uppercase letter to the lowercase letter.

T   o   o

O   o   d

S   o   r

D   o   e

R   o   w

W   o   t

E   o   s

Rhyme Time

Words that rhyme have the same ending sounds. Say the names of the pictures in each row. Circle the two that rhyme.

cat   hat   dog

clock   cake   snake

log   cow   frog

Silly Store

It's time to rhyme again! At this store, there's a star in a jar and a stork with a fork. What other rhyming things do you see?

Color by Words

Trace the words. Then draw lines to match the words that are the same.

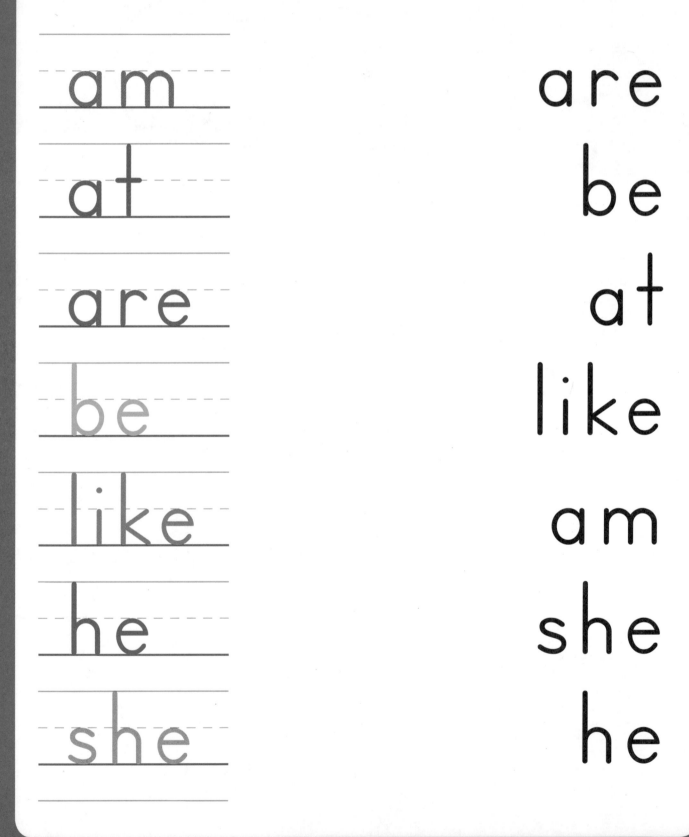

am	are
at	be
are	at
be	like
like	am
he	she
she	he

High-Frequency Words: Sight Words

Color the picture using the word code. What do you see?

WORD CODE

am = brown

at = pink

are = black

be = green

like = blue

he = red

she = orange

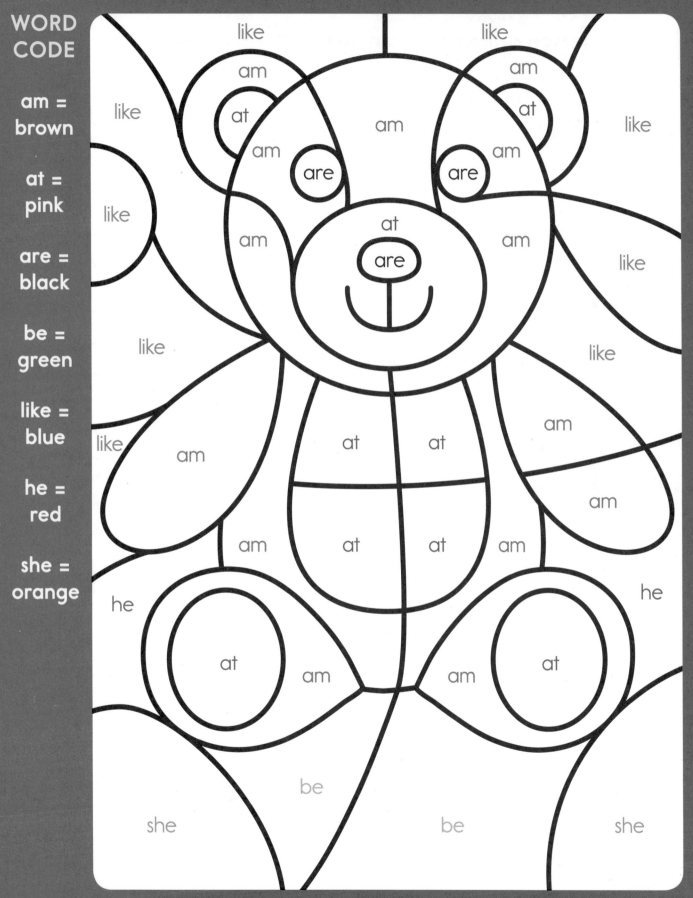

Color by Words

Trace the words. Then draw lines to match the words that are the same.

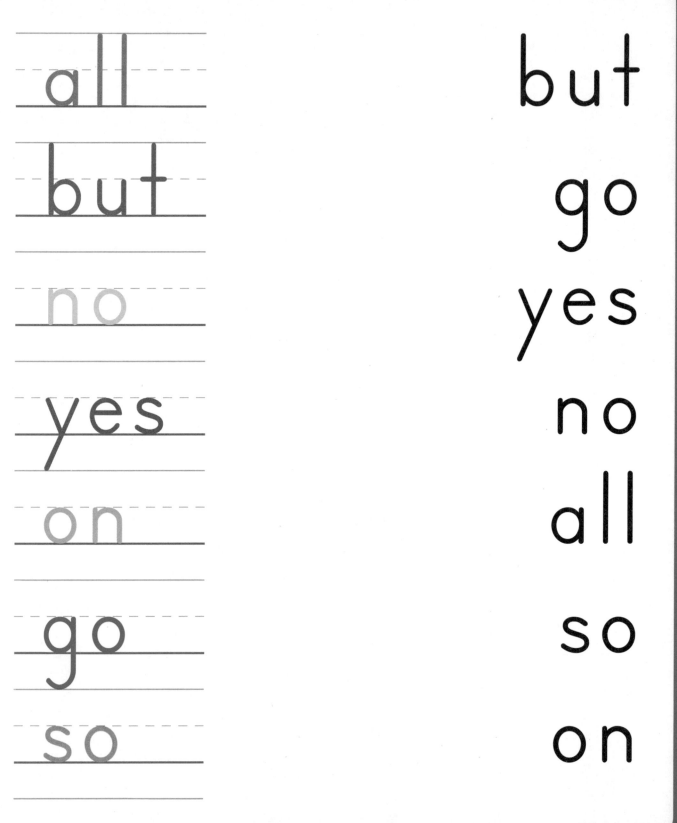

all
but
no
yes
on
go
so

but
go
yes
no
all
so
on

Color the picture using the word code. What do you see?

WORD CODE

all = blue

but = pink

no = yellow

yes = purple

on = green

go = red

so = orange

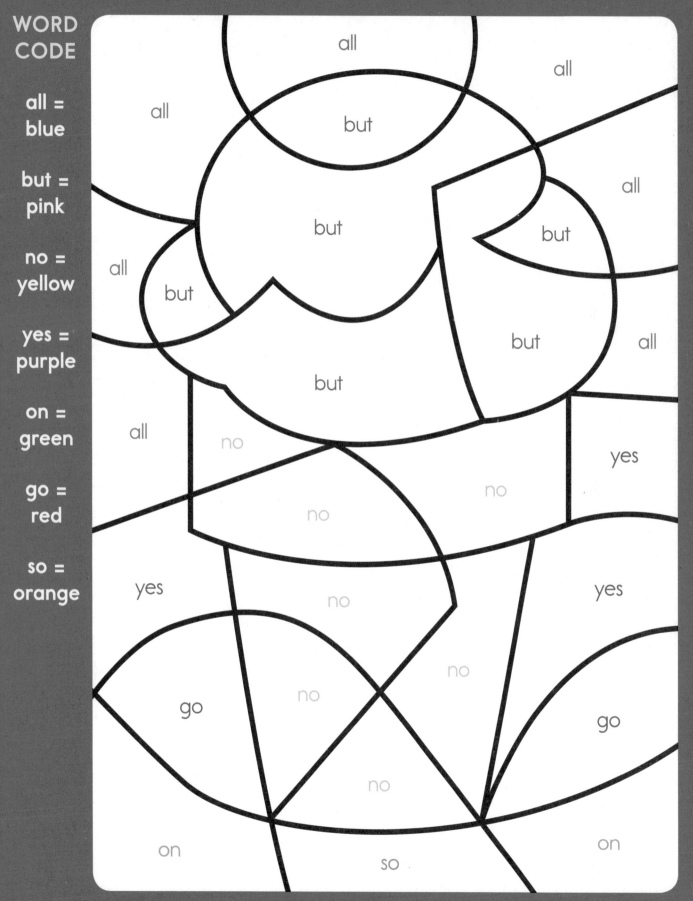

121

Color by Words

Trace the words. Then draw lines to match the words that are the same.

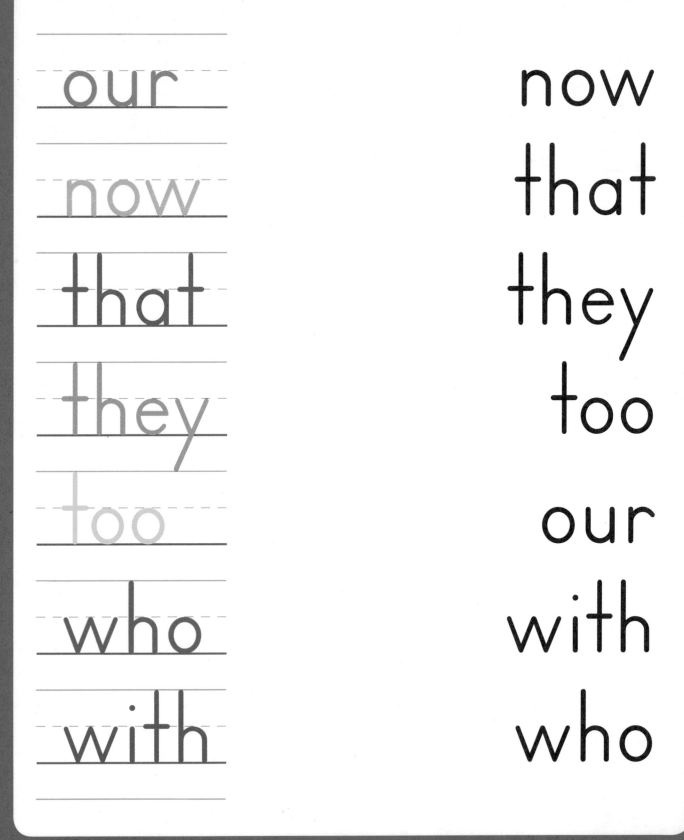

our	now
now	that
that	they
they	too
too	our
who	with
with	who

High-Frequency Words: Sight Words

Color the picture using the word code. What do you see?

WORD CODE

our = blue

now = green

that = red

they = orange

too = yellow

who = purple

with = pink

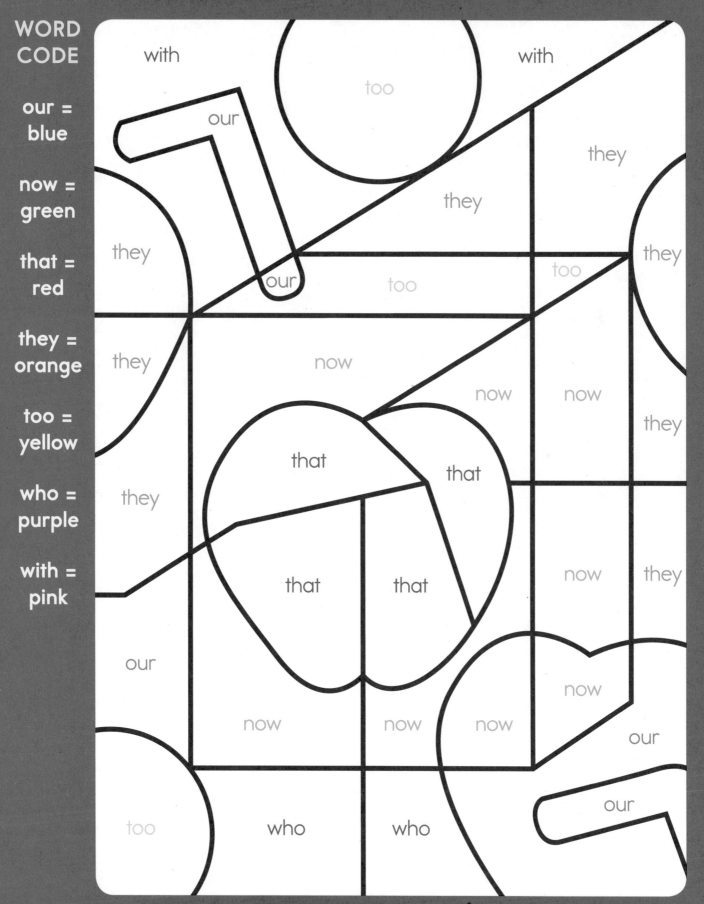

Stop, Watch, and Go!

An Action Rhyme

Traffic light—at the top,
Red light roars, "Stop! Stop! Stop!"

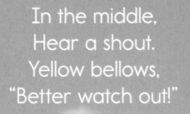

In the middle,
Hear a shout.
Yellow bellows,
"Better watch out!"

At the bottom,
Way down low,

Green light cheers,
"Go! Go! Go!"

Crossing Guard

The crossing guard is helping these students get to school safely.
Find and circle **8** objects in this Hidden Pictures® puzzle.

fork

ghost

baby's bottle

comb

wedge of orange

doughnut

carrot

bowling ball

Time for School!

Visual Discrimination: Describe the Position of Objects

Find the bookcase, cubbies, easel, and reading corner. Tell what each one is near.

What silly things do you see?

Time To Play

Seesaw

Swings

Emergent Writing: Fine Motor Skills

It's recess time. Follow each path to help the kids get to the playground.

What do you like to do at the playground?

Climbing Net

Slide

Painting a Rainbow

All my favorite colors
   are painted way up high.
They make a bridge that I pretend
   to climb up to the sky.
And when I reach the middle,
   I take a little ride.
I slide right down
   that rainbow bridge to
   reach the other side.

High-Frequency Words: Color Words

Ryan is painting a rainbow. Find the objects in the picture that match the colors in the rainbow.

The colors in a rainbow are red, orange, yellow, green, blue, and purple.

Fun in the Sun

Find and circle **6** objects in this Hidden Pictures® puzzle.

Color the apples **red.** Color the giraffes yellow.
Color the tree leaves green. Color the sky **blue.**

ice-cream
cone

bell

scissors

toothbrush

lamp

baseball
cap

Trace each color word. Then write your own.

red

yellow

green

blue

Fun in the Rain

Find and circle **6** objects in this Hidden Pictures® puzzle.

Color the rain boots orange. Color the umbrella **purple**.
Color the cat **black**. Color the dogs **brown**.

ghost

envelope

ball of yarn

slice of
lemon

paper
bag

flag

Trace each color word. Then write your own.

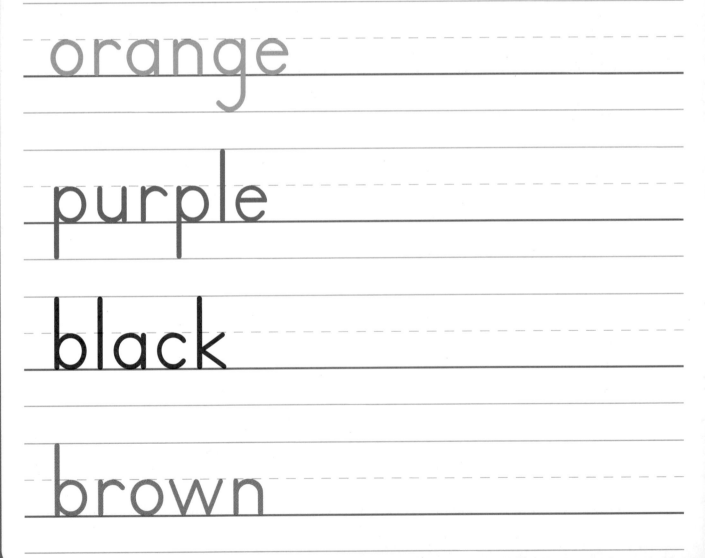

orange

purple

black

brown

That's Silly!™

red

orange

yellow

green

blue

purple

brown

black

High-Frequency Words: Color Words

Trace each color word. Draw a line from each word to something that matches that color.

What silly things do you see?

The Shapes' Picnic

The shapes all decided one beautiful day
That they'd have a picnic down by the bay.
They would meet at noon and
Bring something to munch.
They'd relax and have fun
With a nice picnic lunch.

Read the story. What shapes do you see?

Square brought sandwiches on toasted rye.
Triangle came with slices of pie.

Rectangle came with juice boxes to share.
Oval brought watermelon—plenty to spare.

But where was Circle? He was not to be found.
"Maybe he's looking for something that's round!"

Then all of a sudden,
Dark clouds rolled,
Rain came down,
And the air felt cold.

"Our picnic is ruined!"
The shapes all cried.

"Don't worry," said Circle,
Who had finally arrived.

Reading: Story; Geometry: Shapes

The soggy shapes said,
"This picnic's NOT fun!"

"But look," said Circle.
"I brought the sun!"

Circle

A circle is round.
Trace the circle.

Draw a circle
on your own.

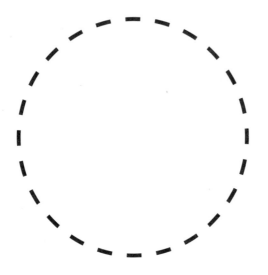

Look at the objects below. Color all the circles that you see.

Square

A square has 4 sides that are the same size. Trace the square.

Draw a square on your own.

Look at the objects below. Color all the squares that you see.

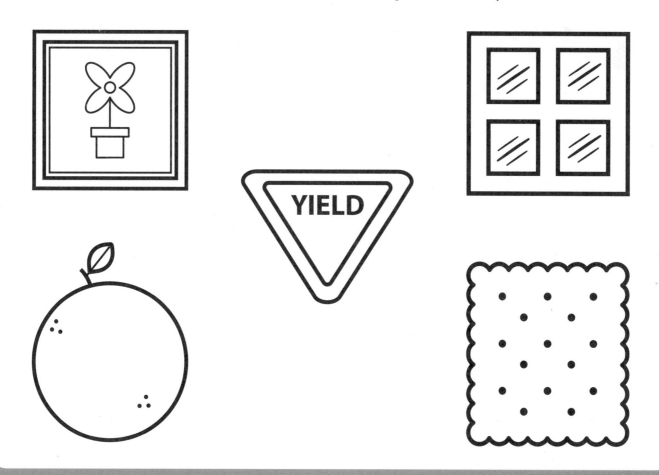

Triangle

A triangle has 3 sides. Trace the triangle.

Draw a triangle on your own.

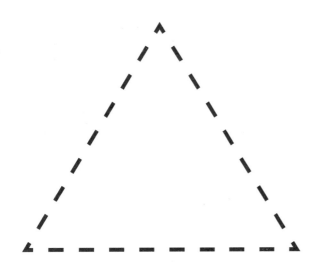

Look at the objects below. Color all the triangles that you see.

Rectangle

A rectangle has 2 long sides and 2 short sides. Trace the rectangle.

Draw a rectangle on your own.

Look at the objects below. Color all the rectangles that you see.

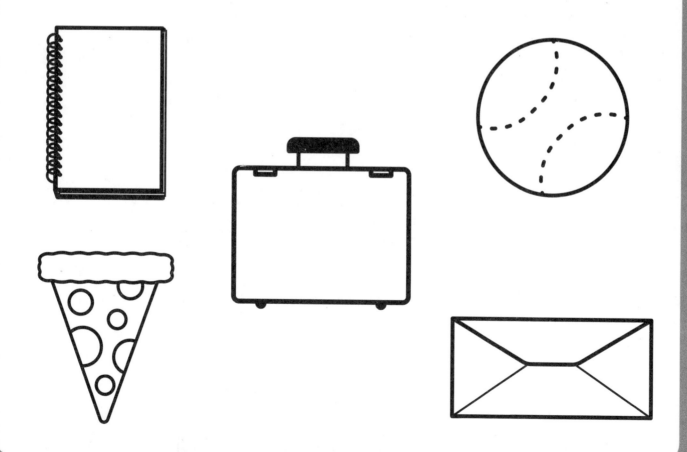

Rhombus

A rhombus is like a stretched square. Trace the rhombus.

Draw a rhombus on your own.

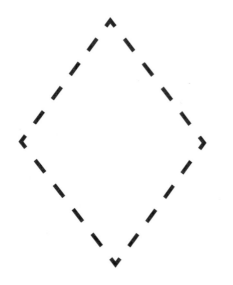

Look at the objects below. Color all the rhombuses that you see.

Oval

An oval is like a stretched circle. Trace the oval.

Draw an oval on your own.

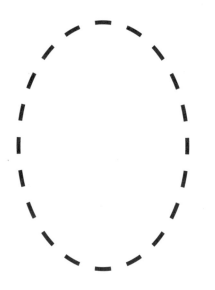

Look at the objects below. Color all the ovals that you see.

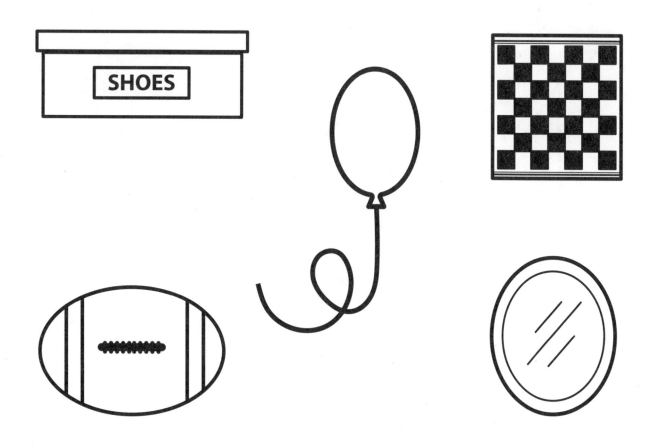

Shape Hunt

What shapes do you see? Look for ☐ squares, ▭ rectangles, △ triangles, ◯ circles, ⬭ ovals, and ◇ rhombuses in this picture.

149

0 zero

This is the number 0.

This is the word **zero**.

This is one way to show 0.

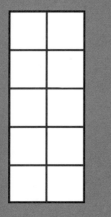

Trace the number **0**. Then write your own.

Trace the word **zero**. Then write your own.

zero

This garden has **0** flowers in it.

Circle the pots that have **0** flowers in them.

I

one

This is the
number I.

This is the
word **one**.

This is
one way
to show I.

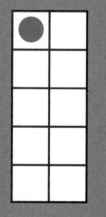

Trace the number I. Then write your own.

Trace the word **one**. Then write your own.

one

Can you find I squirrel?
I cat? I birdhouse? I snail?

What else do you see?

2

two

This is the number 2.

This is the word two.

This is one way to show 2.

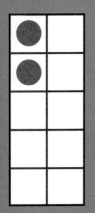

Trace the number **2**. Then write your own.

2 2 2

Trace the word **two**. Then write your own.

two

Abby's **2** feet take her skipping down the street.

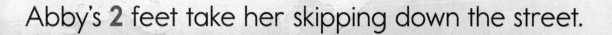

What things in sets of **2** do you see?

3
three

This is the number 3.

This is the word **three**.

This is one way to show 3.

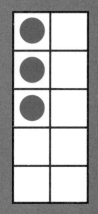

Trace the number **3**. Then write your own.

3 3

Trace the word **three**. Then write your own.

three

These **3** little kitty cats lost their favorite hats. Can you help them find **3** hats?

What things in groups of **3** do you see?

4
four

This is the number 4.

This is the word **four**.

This is one way to show 4.

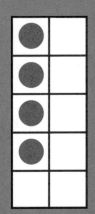

Trace the number **4**. Then write your own.

Trace the word **four**. Then write your own.

BAKERY

STOP

NUG14-3

It's a **4**-way stop. How many cars do you see? How many trucks do you see?

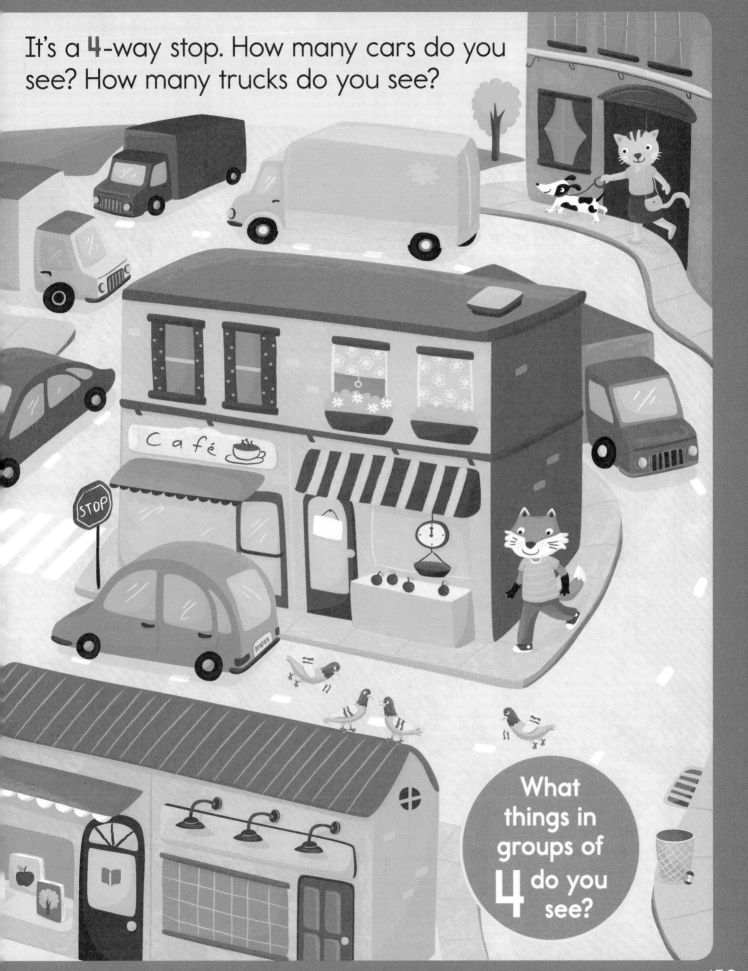

What things in groups of **4** do you see?

5
five

This is the number **5**.

This is the word **five**.

This is one way to show **5**.

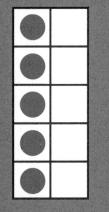

Trace the number **5**. Then write your own.

5 5

Trace the word **five**. Then write your own.

five

It's time to set the table for these **5** family members.

What things in groups of **5** do you see?

Countdown: 5 to 1

If you were an astronaut, what would you take with you to outer space?

Can you find **5** planets, **4** shooting stars, **3** aliens, **2** moons, and I sun?

6

six

This is the number 6.

This is the word six.

This is one way to show 6.

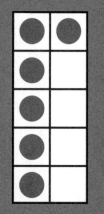

Trace the number **6**. Then write your own.

6 6

Trace the word **six**. Then write your own.

six

Sophie has **6** buttons on her coat.

What things in groups of **6** do you see?

7

seven

This is the number 7.

This is the word **seven**.

This is one way to show 7.

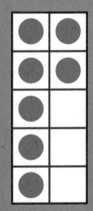

Trace the number **7**. Then write your own.

Trace the word **seven**. Then write your own.

seven

There are **7** sailors on the deck of this ship.

What things in groups of 7 do you see?

8
eight

This is the number 8.

This is the word **eight**.

This is one way to show 8.

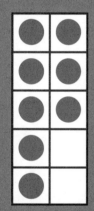

Trace the number **8**. Then write your own.

8

Trace the word **eight**. Then write your own.

eight

This octopus has **8** hats.

What things in groups of **8** do you see?

9
nine

This is the number 9.

This is the word **nine**.

This is one way to show 9.

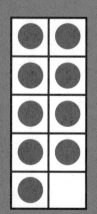

Trace the number **9**. Then write your own.

Trace the word **nine**. Then write your own.

nine

These 9 students are enjoying their lunches.

What things in groups of 9 do you see?

10
ten

This is the number 10.

This is the word **ten**.

This is one way to show 10.

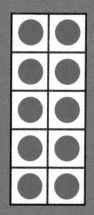

Trace the number **10**. Then write your own.

10 10

Trace the word **ten**. Then write your own.

ten

What things in groups of 10 do you see?

These 10 sheep are going to bed.

Can you find **10** squirrels, **9** red birds, **8** snowmen, **7** green trees, and **6** kids?

11

eleven

This is the number 11.

This is the word **eleven**.

This is one way to show 11.

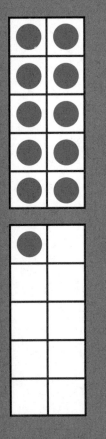

Trace the number 11. Then write your own.

Trace the word **eleven**.

eleven

Count the 11 balloons. Then draw a design on the biggest balloon.

12
twelve

This is the number 12.

This is the word **twelve**.

This is one way to show 12.

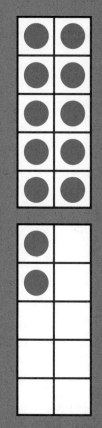

Trace the number **12**. Then write your own.

12   12

Trace the word **twelve**.

twelve

Count the 12 birds. Can you think of other words that start with *b*?

13
thirteen

This is the number 13.

This is the word thirteen.

This is one way to show 13.

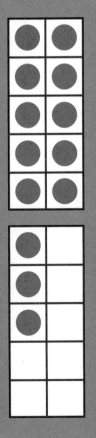

Trace the number **13**. Then write your own.

13 13

Trace the word **thirteen**.

thirteen

Count the 13 kids. Then circle the kids wearing yellow.

14

fourteen

This is the number 14.

This is the word fourteen.

This is one way to show 14.

Trace the number 14. Then write your own.

1 2 3

14

Trace the word **fourteen**.

fourteen

Count the 14 dinosaurs. Which game would you like to play? Why?

15
fifteen

This is the number 15.

This is the word fifteen.

This is one way to show 15.

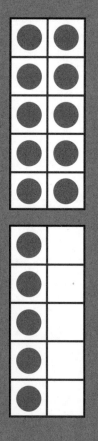

Trace the number 15. Then write your own.

Trace the word **fifteen**.

Count the 15 trucks. Can you think of other words that start with *t*?

16
sixteen

This is the number 16.

This is the word sixteen.

This is one way to show 16.

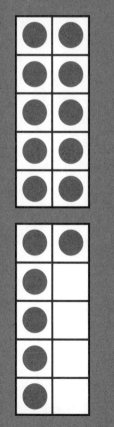

Trace the number 16. Then write your own.

16 16

Trace the word **sixteen**.

sixteen

Count the 16 leaves. Draw a line between each matching pair.

17

seventeen

This is the number 17.

This is the word seventeen.

This is one way to show 17.

Trace the number 17. Then write your own.

17 17

Trace the word **seventeen**.

seventeen

Count the 17 mittens. Can you think of a word that rhymes with *mittens*?

18

eighteen

This is the number 18.

This is the word **eighteen**.

This is one way to show 18.

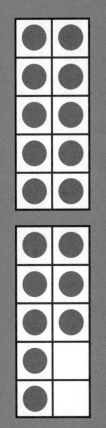

Trace the number **18**. Then write your own.

18 18

Trace the word **eighteen**.

eighteen

Count the 18 chicks. Then circle the yellow ones.

19
nineteen

This is the number 19.

This is the word nineteen.

This is one way to show 19.

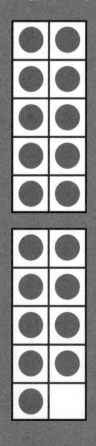

Trace the number 19. Then write your own.

19 19

Trace the word **nineteen**.

nineteen

Count the 19 worms. Can you think of other words that start with w?

20
twenty

This is the number 20.

This is the word twenty.

This is one way to show 20.

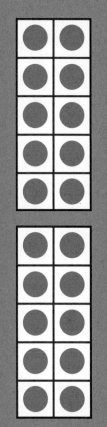

Trace the number **20**. Then write your own.

20 20

Trace the word **twenty**.

twenty

Count the 20 fish. What other animals live in water?

11 to 20

Write the numbers next to the number words.

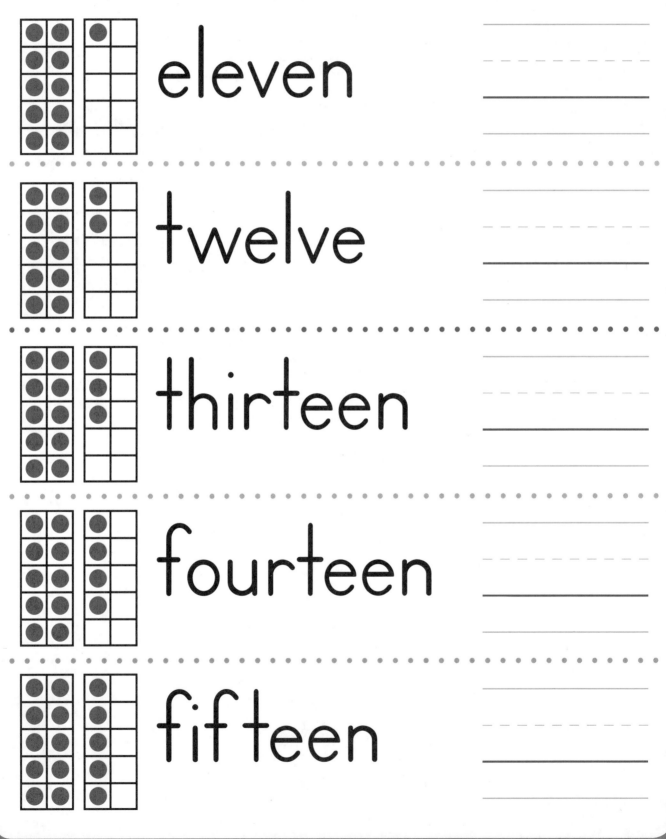

eleven _____

twelve _____

thirteen _____

fourteen _____

fifteen _____

Write the numbers next to the number words.

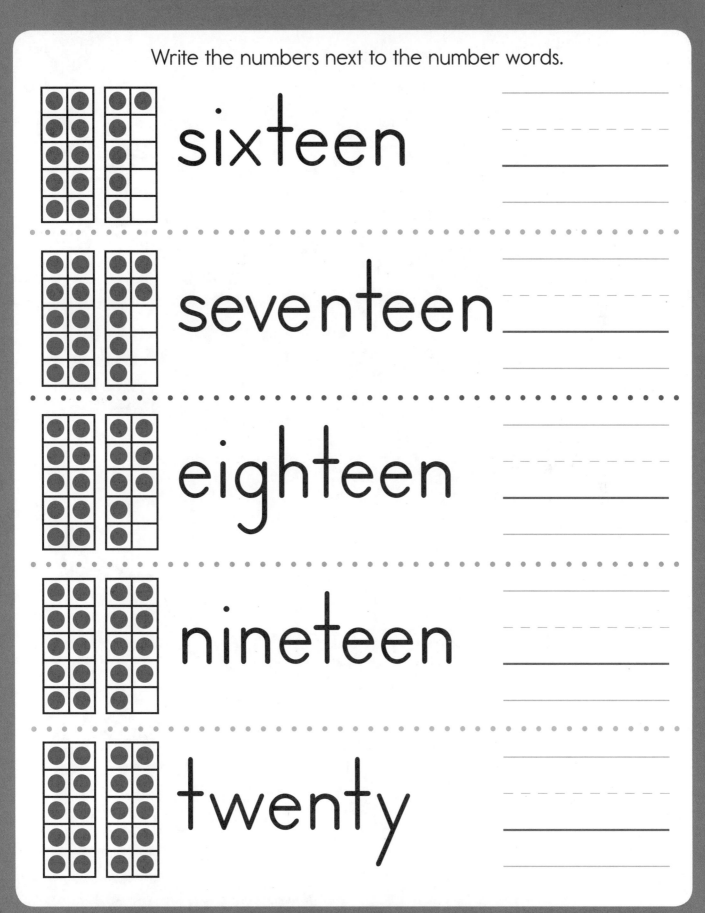

sixteen

seventeen

eighteen

nineteen

twenty

Bug Fill-In

Write the missing numbers.

[ ] 2 [ ] [ ] 5
6
[ ] 8 [ ]
10
[ ]
12
13 [ ] [ ] 16
[ ]
18
20 [ ]

How are these pictures the same? How are they different?

Write the missing numbers.

Floating Fill-In

Write the missing numbers.

Count by 2's

Count by 2's to fill in the missing numbers.

2, 4, ___, ___, 10,

___, 14, ___, ___, 20

4, ___, ___, 8, ___,

12, ___, 16, 18, ___

Count by 3's

Count by 3's to fill in the missing numbers.

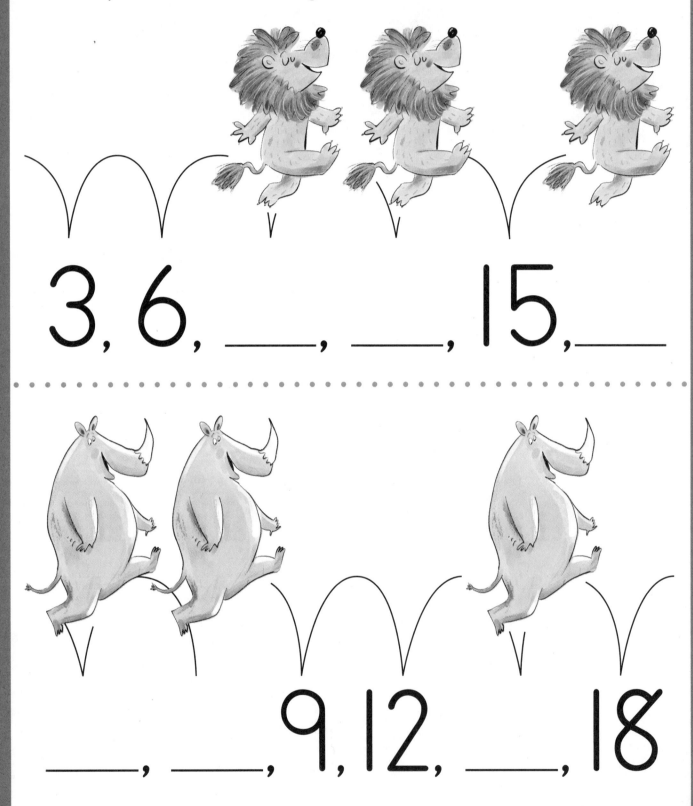

3, 6, ___, ___, 15, ___

___, ___, 9, 12, ___, 18

Count by 4's

Count by 4's to fill in the missing numbers.

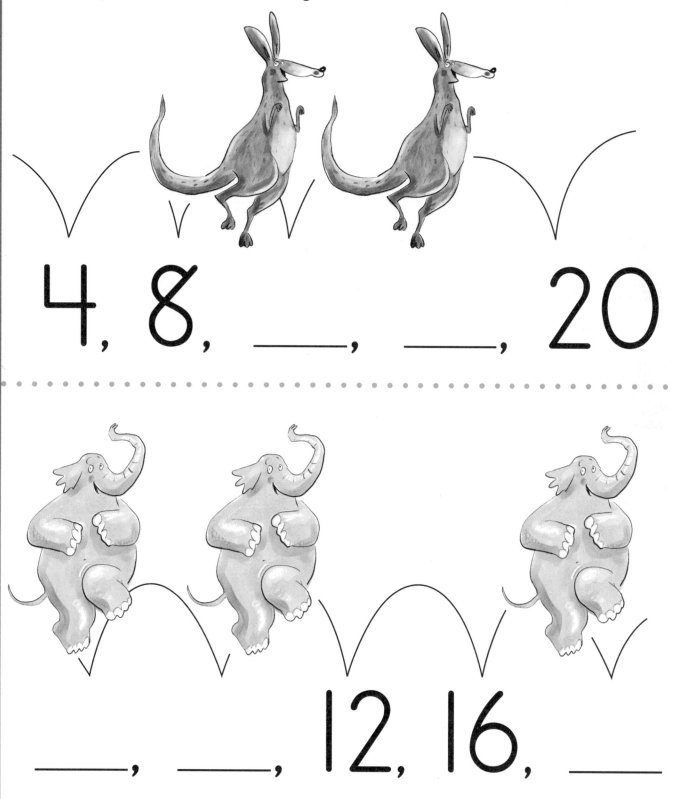

4, 8, ____, ____, 20

____, ____, 12, 16, ____

Shape Patterns

Which shape comes next? Draw the shape that completes the pattern in each row.

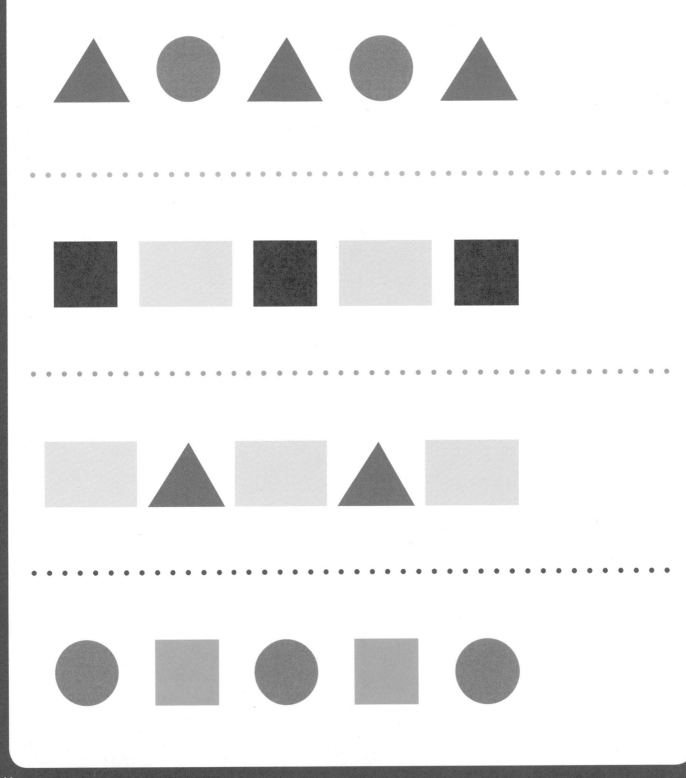

Mathematical Thinking: Patterns

Robot Patterns

Which color comes next? Color the white robots to complete the pattern in each row.

Pattern Mazes

Follow this pattern to help the lamb get to her mama.

Follow this pattern to help the penguin get to his dad.

Bedtime Patterns

Find and circle these **8** objects in the Hidden Pictures® puzzle.

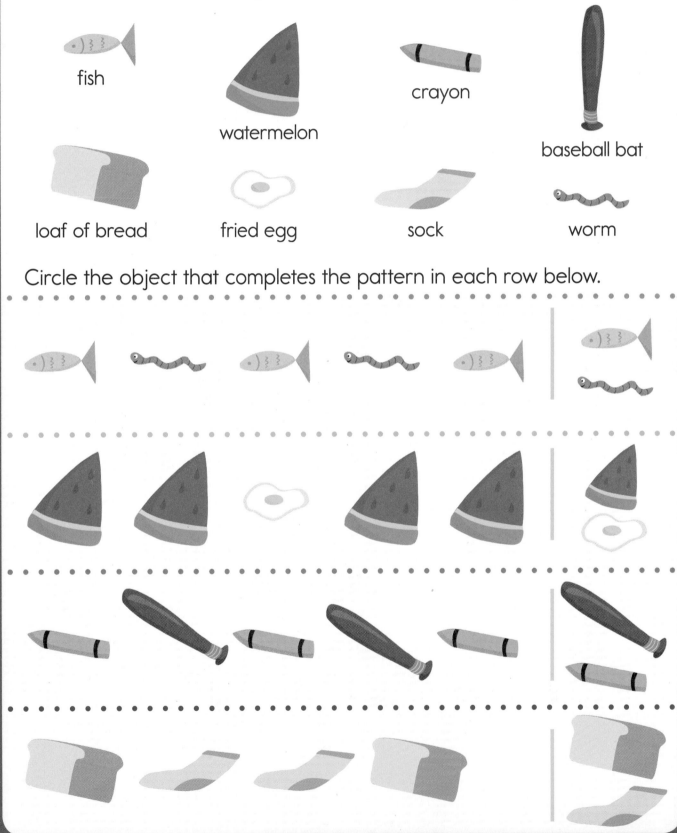

fish

watermelon

crayon

baseball bat

loaf of bread

fried egg

sock

worm

Circle the object that completes the pattern in each row below.

What patterns do you see in this scene?

We Go Together

Match each pair of objects that are used together.

backpack

paint

desk

hook

pencil

chair

books

easel

sharpener

coat

Match each object to the helper who uses it.

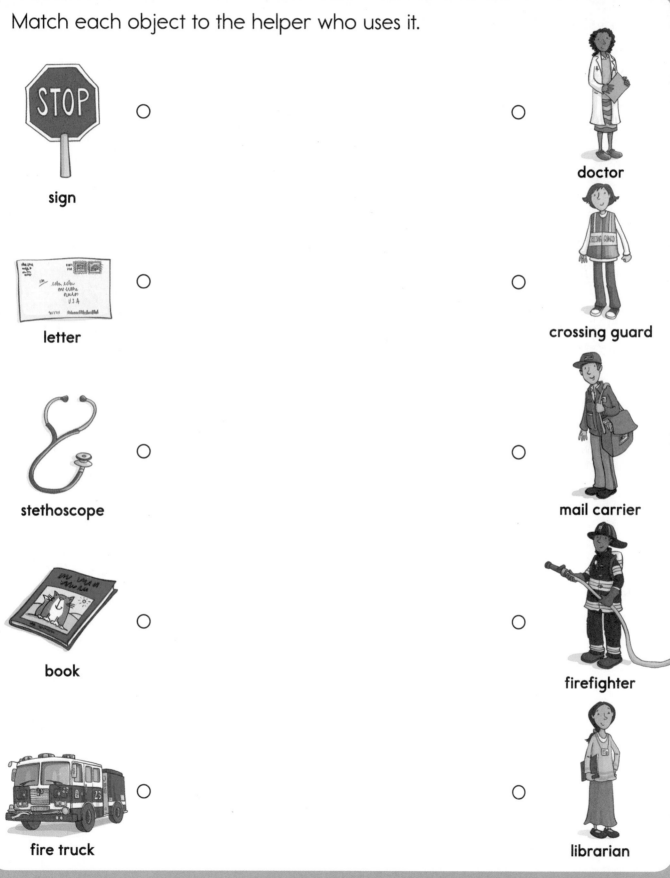

sign

letter

stethoscope

book

fire truck

doctor

crossing guard

mail carrier

firefighter

librarian

What Doesn't Belong?

Cross out the object in each group that doesn't belong with the others.

Cross out the object in each group that doesn't belong with the others.

Same Snowboarders

Cross out the snowboarder that is different in each row.

Visual Discrimination: Similarities and Differences

Ladybug Spots

Draw spots on the ladybugs on the right to make them match the ones on the left.

Art Class

Visual Discrimination: Similarities and Differences

How are these pictures the same? How are they different?

Big Bath

Circle the biggest object in each row. Then find and circle these **5** objects in this Hidden Pictures® puzzle.

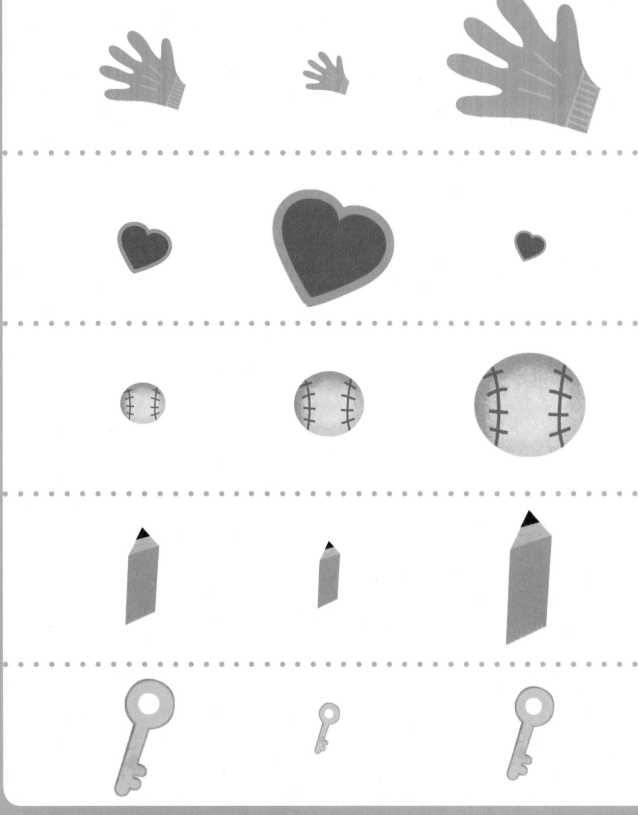

Big and Small

Circle the biggest kangaroo.

Circle the smallest fish.

Long and Short

Circle the longest crocodile.

Circle the shortest flamingo.

Tall and Short

Circle the tallest giraffe.

Circle the shortest penguin.

Small and Large

Circle the smallest crab.

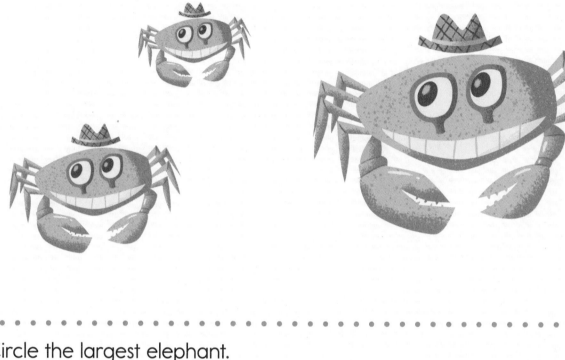

Circle the largest elephant.

That's Silly!™

Find each pair of opposites.

slow
fast
out
in
wet
dry
above
below
light
heavy
over
closed
open
under

What silly things do you see?

Opposites

Hot and cold are opposites. Which picture shows hot weather?
Which picture shows cold weather? How can you tell?
Find and circle **8** objects in this Hidden Pictures® puzzle.

flip-flop

pliers

pencil

orange

sailboat

cinnamon bun

magnifying glass

tire

Night and *day* are opposites. Which picture shows night?
Which picture shows day? How can you tell?
Find and circle **8** objects in this Hidden Pictures® puzzle.

cap

saltshaker

fork

mitten

fishhook

clover

slice of cake

wishbone

More Opposites

Quiet and *loud* are opposites. Which picture shows a loud place? Which picture shows a quiet place? How can you tell? Find and circle **8** objects in this Hidden Pictures® puzzle.

ladder

banana

umbrella

dinosaur

sunglasses

spider

star

wristwatch

Big and *small* are opposites. Can you find examples of something big and something small in these pictures? What other opposites do you see? Find and circle **8** objects in this Hidden Pictures® puzzle.

comb

pliers

saucepan

fish

crayon

umbrella

football

feather

More or Less

Circle the group in each row that has more cats.

Counting: Compare Groups

The symbol < means **less than**.

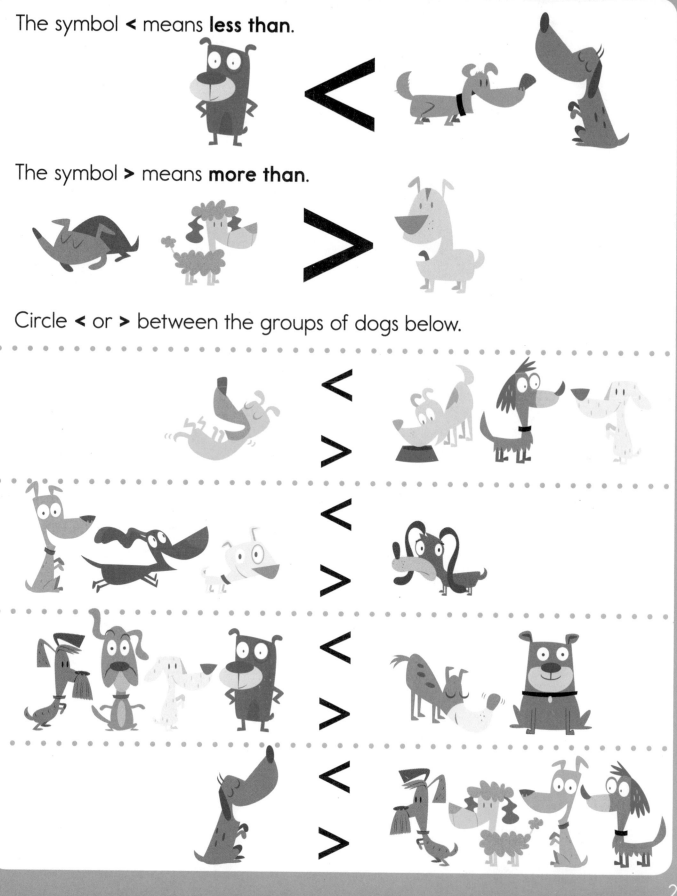

The symbol > means **more than**.

Circle < or > between the groups of dogs below.

More or Less

Count the school supplies in each group. Write the number in the space beside it. Circle **<** or **>** to show what number in each row is more or less.

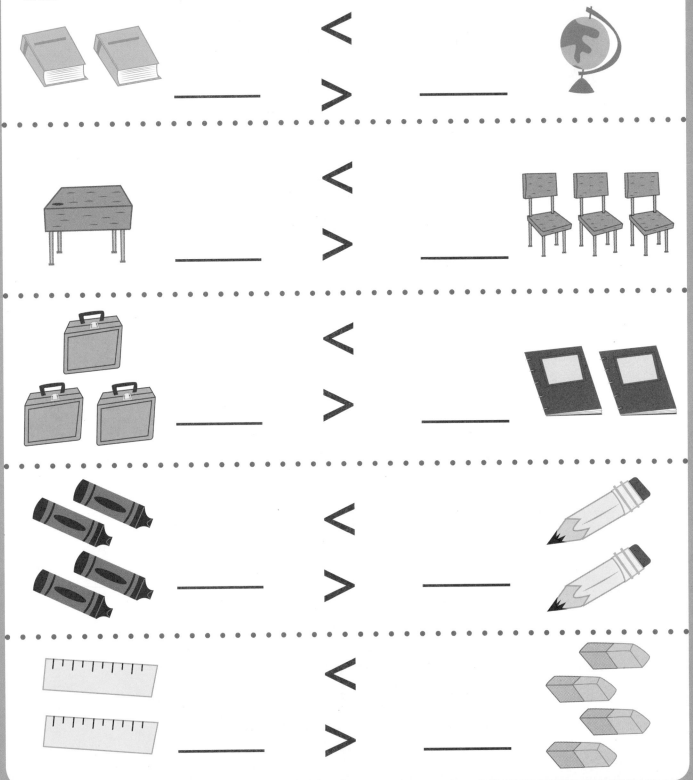

How many books do you see in each pile? Color in a square for every book that you see. Then circle the pile with more books.

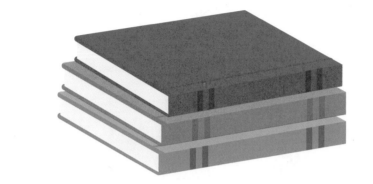

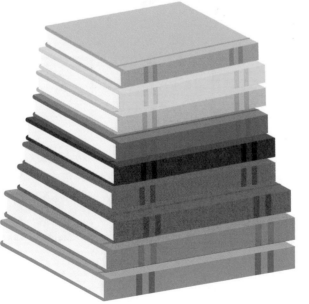

More or Less

How many bananas do you see in each tray? Color in a square for every banana that you see. Then circle the tray with more bananas.

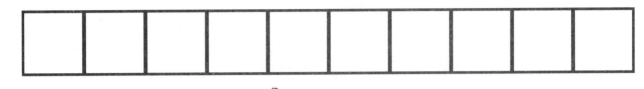

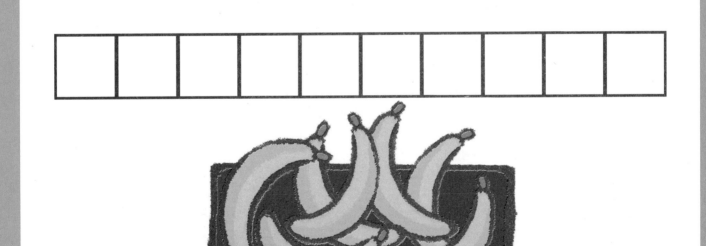

How many apples do you see in each bin? Color in a square for every apple that you see. Then circle the bin with the the most apples.

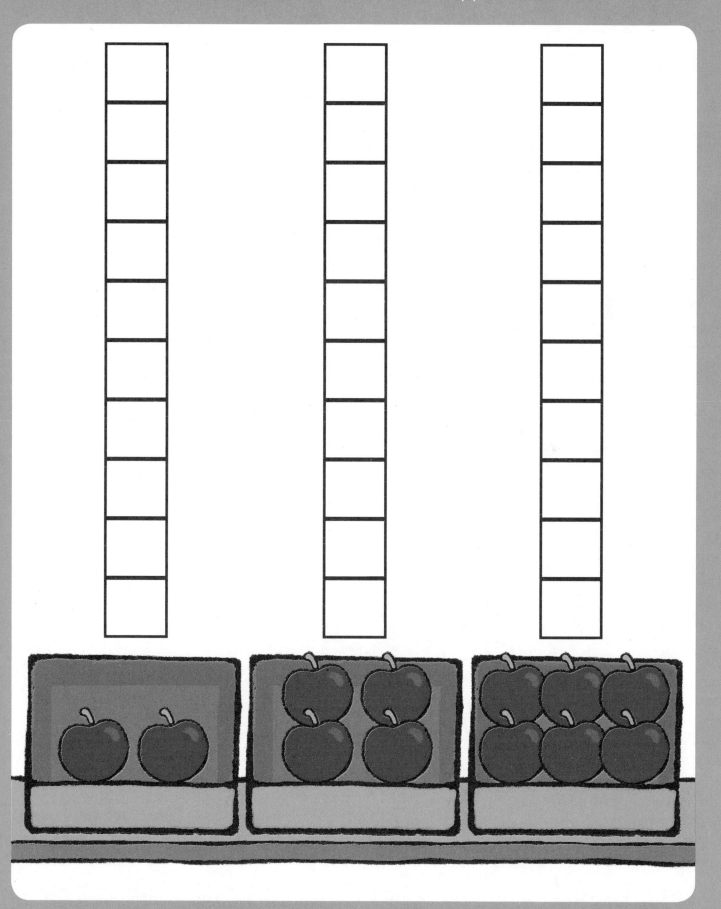

Happy Birthday!

Draw candles on the cake to show how old you are.

Counting: Numbers and Quantities

How old were you one year ago? Circle the number of cupcakes that show how old you were.

How old will you be in one year? Circle the number of cupcakes that show how old you will be.

Draw a line from each cupcake to its match.

Fish Addition

Count the fish in the first fishbowl and write the number. Count the fish in the second fishbowl and write the number. How many fish are in both fishbowls?

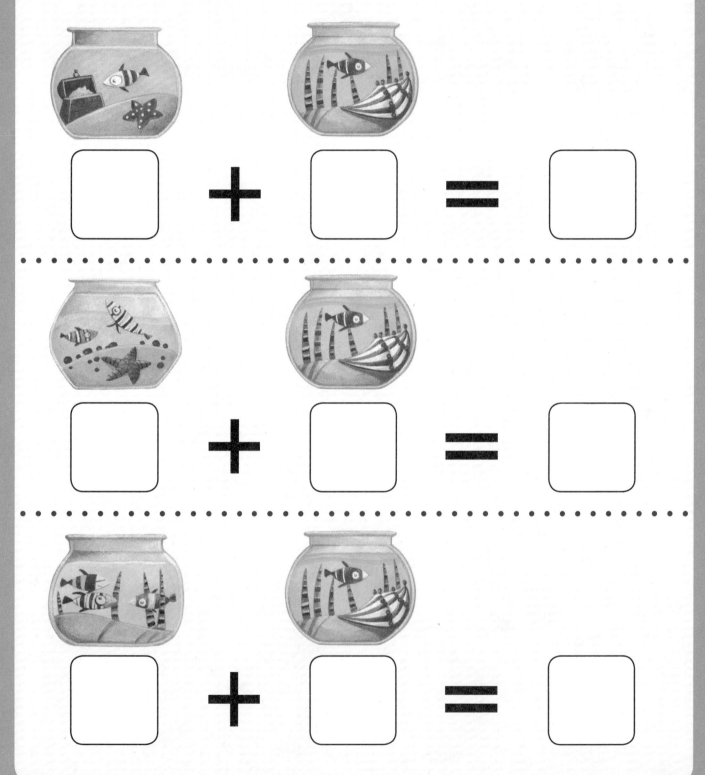

Monster Addition

Count the eyes on the first monster and write the number. Count the eyes on the second monster and write the number. How many eyes are on both monsters?

Kite Addition

Count the bows on the first kite tail and write the number. Count the bows on the second kite tail and write the number. How many bows are on both kites?

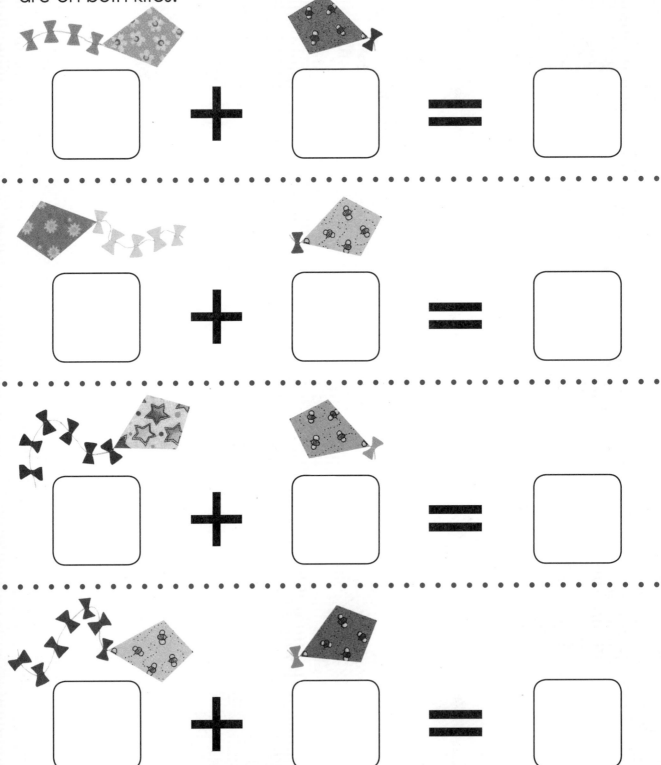

Pig Addition

Count the pigs in the first group and write the number. Count the pigs in the second group and write the number. How many pigs are in both groups?

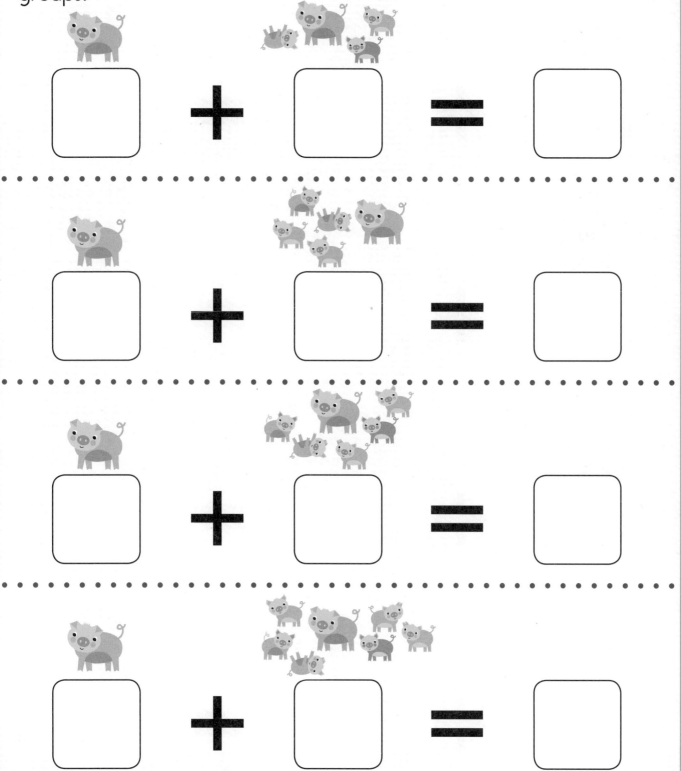

Bug Addition

Count the bugs on the first leaf and write the number. Count the bugs on the second leaf and write the number. How many bugs are on both leaves?

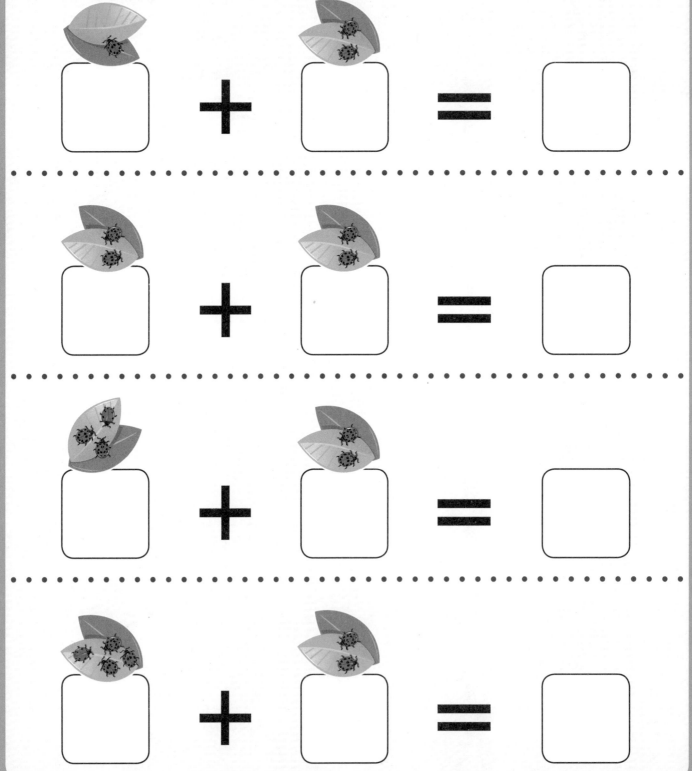

Cow Addition

Count the cows in the first group and write the number. Count the cows in the second group and write the number. How many cows are in both groups?

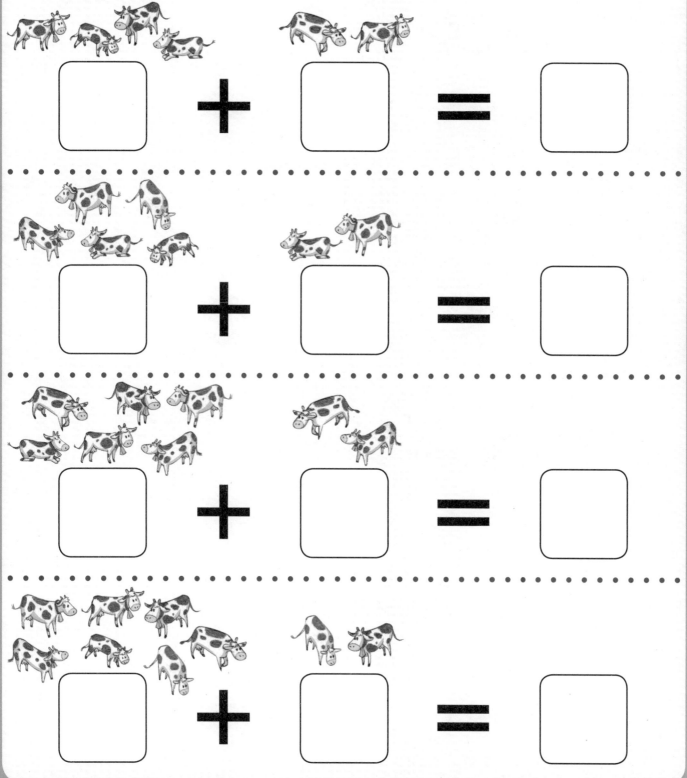

Boat Subtraction

Count the boats in each group and write the number. Count how many are crossed off and write the number. How many boats are left? We did one to get you started.

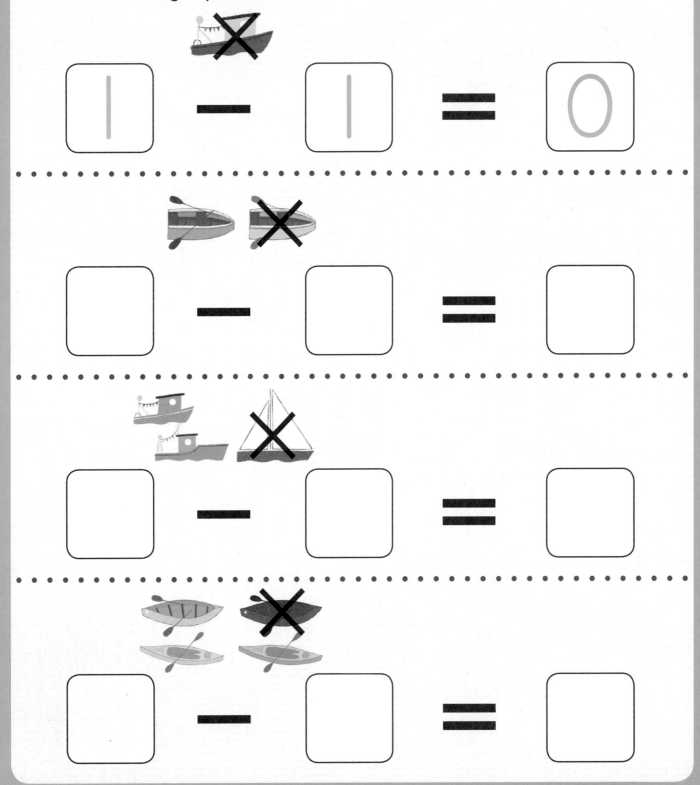

$1 - 1 = 0$

Pizza Subtraction

Count the slices of pizza in each group and write the number. Count how many are crossed off and write the number. How many slices are left? We did one to get you started.

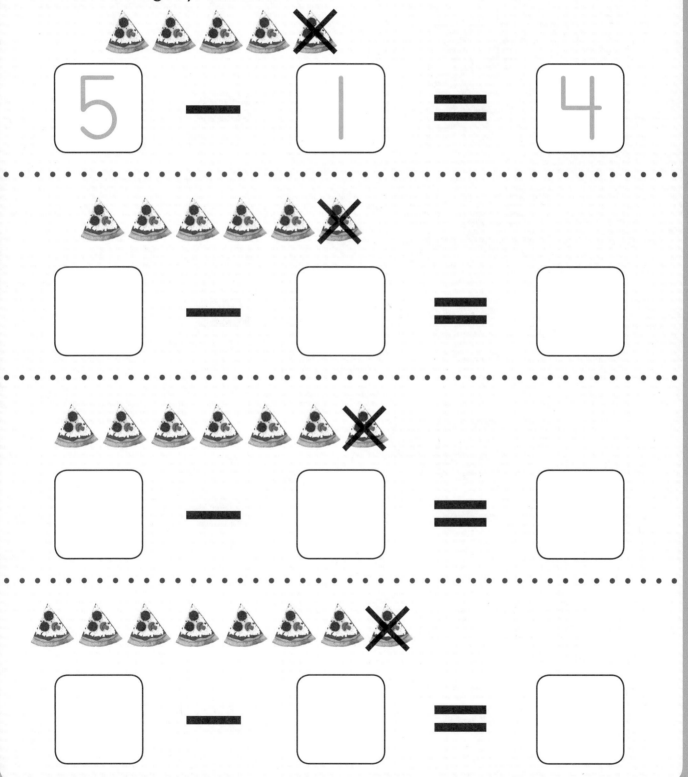

5 − 1 = 4

☐ − ☐ = ☐

☐ − ☐ = ☐

☐ − ☐ = ☐

Sock Subtraction

Count the socks in each group and write the number. Count how many are crossed off and write the number. How many socks are left? We did one to get you started.

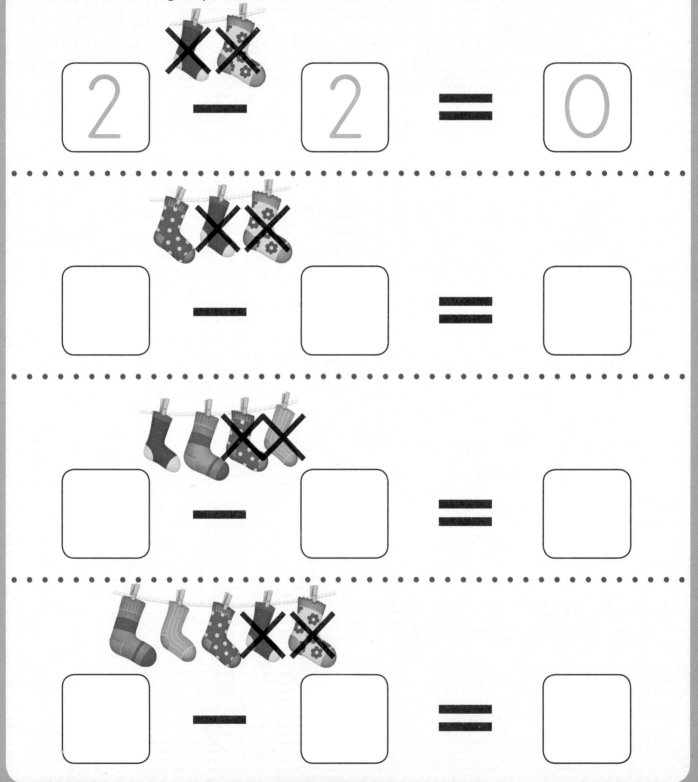

2 − 2 = 0

☐ − ☐ = ☐

☐ − ☐ = ☐

☐ − ☐ = ☐

Apple Subtraction

Count the apples in each group and write the number. Count how many are crossed off and write the number. How many apples are left? We did one to get you started.

Bird Subtraction

Count the birds in each group and write the number. Count how many are crossed off and write the number. How many birds are left? We did one to get you started.

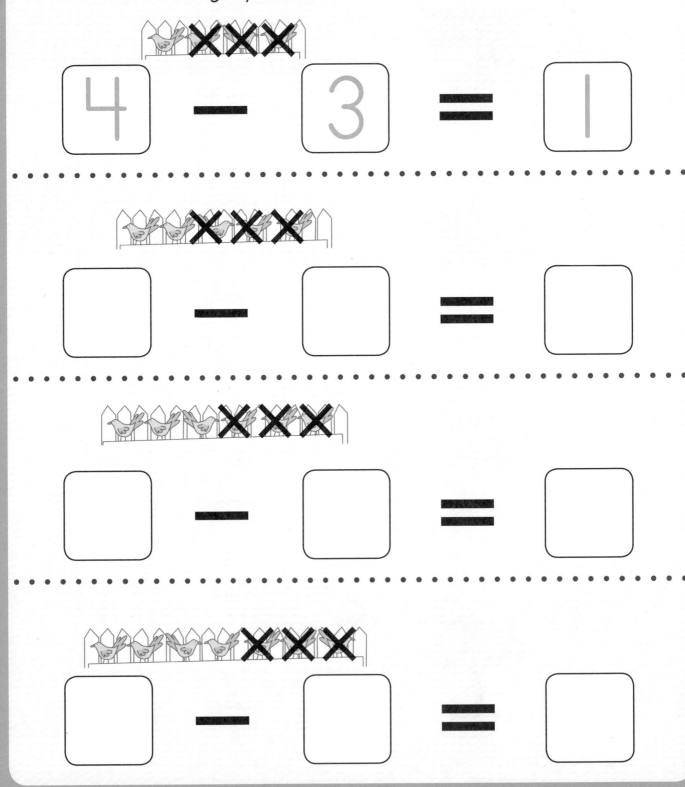

$$4 - 3 = 1$$

Flower Subtraction

Count the flowers in each group and write the number. Count how many are crossed off and write the number. How many flowers are left? We did one to get you started.

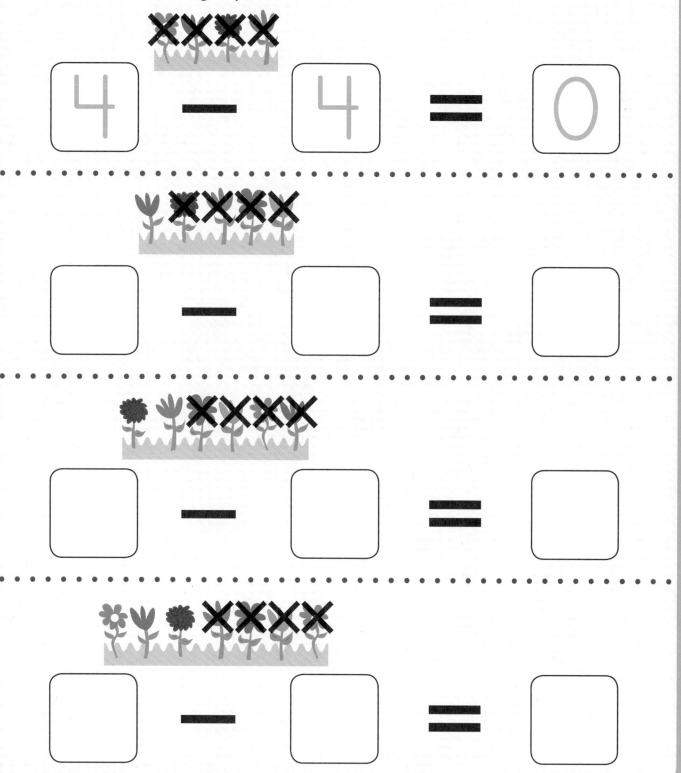

4 − 4 = 0

My Day

 Circle what you do in the morning.

Circle what you do at school.

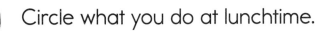 Circle what you do at lunchtime.

Circle what you do in the afternoon.

Circle what you do in the evening.

Circle what you do at night.

Greenfoot Gus

Greenfoot Gus went off to school,
went off to school one day.
He couldn't wait to read and write,
to count and paint and play.

"Dum-dum, dee-doe. It's off I go!
I'm off to school," he sang.

But by the time he got to school—
ding-dong!—the last bell rang.
"Dum-dum, dee-dee, that won't stop me!"
sang little Greenfoot Gus.

Reading: Story

The next day he went off to school.
He rode there on the bus!

Building with Blocks

These pictures are all mixed up. Put them in order. Use **1**, **2**, and **3** to show the order.

Draw your very own block tower.

Sliding Down

These pictures are all mixed up. Put them in order. Use **1**, **2**, and **3** to show the order.

Draw a picture of yourself going down this slide.

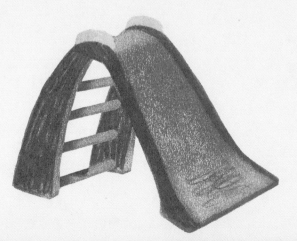

Making a Pizza

These pictures are all mixed up. Put them in order. Use **1**, **2**, **3**, and **4** to show the order.

Draw your favorite toppings on this pizza.

Relate Ideas: Sequence Pictures

Growing Watermelons

These pictures are all mixed up. Put them in order. Use **1**, **2**, **3**, and **4** to show the order.

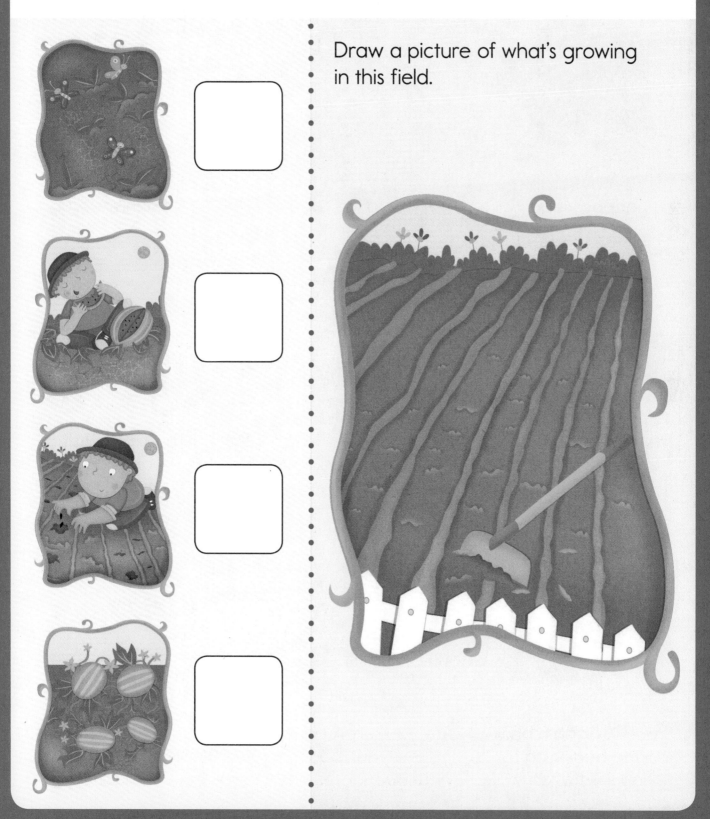

Draw a picture of what's growing in this field.

Scavenger Hunt

Hooray for this
happy hippo!

Follow a pattern
to find this robot.

Follow the Z's to
find this zebra.

This dinosaur is playing
a number of games
with his friends.

This lamp will light
the way.

This silly octopus
is driving an
orange car.

Trace your path back
to the beginning to
find this butterfly.

Are you surprised to see
this silly surfboarding
snowman again?

What shapes make up
this ice-cream cone?

Use the hints to find each of these objects in the book. What was your favorite puzzle?

This D-lightful dog is at a dog park.

What time of day do you have recess?

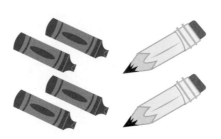

Are there more crayons or pencils to find?

Pepperoni pizza, please!

This snowboarder is different from the others.

This sign may be a familiar sight on your way to school.

This skipping rhino is skipping numbers.

Where can we find wiggling worms?

These 3 plants are with other groups of 3.

Answers

Page 12
Awesome Acrobats

Page 28
Eggs for Everyone

Page 40
Hannah's Hairbrush

Page 48
Juggling Jesters

Page 64
Neat Newts

Page 84
School Surprise

Page 92
Umbrella Search

Page 104
Double X-Rays

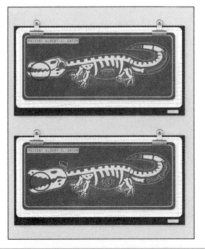

Page 108
Yo-Yo Search

Answers

Page 209
Big Bath

Page 216
Opposites

Page 217
Opposites

Page 218
Opposites

Page 219
Opposites

Inside Front Cover

Pages 250–251
Scavenger Hunt

Inside Back Cover

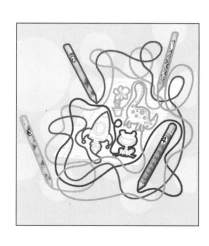

Highlights™

Congratulations!

(your name)

worked hard
and finished the

Kindergarten
Big Fun Workbook

That's Silly!™

What silly things do you see?